Praise for *The Healing Art of Storytelling*

"It is by learning to *listen* to one another and by sharing our stories that we discover our shared humanity. Each one of us, both within our own families and communities, as well as among those of different faiths, traditions and even ancient enmities, needs urgently to be heard if healing is to be found. Richard Stone's book sets out how each of us may make a start in a practical as well as inspirational way."

—James Roose-Evans, author of *Passages of the Soul: Ritual Today*, and award-winning director of *84 Charing Cross Road*

"Richard Stone is a consumate storyteller and teacher. With grace he guides us into the healing process: remembering ourselves, speaking our truth, and finding ultimate meaning in telling our story. *The Healing Art of Storytelling* has already become a rich resource for GETTING WELL: A Mind/Body Health Program for Individuals with Life-Challenging Conditions."

—Deirdre Davis Brigham, founder of GETTING WELL, Orlando, Fla., and author of *Imagery for Getting Well*

"In *The Healing Art of Storytelling*, Richard Stone has created a wondrous blend of vibrant story and his own step-by-step approach to making effective story a part of your own life. His examples are nearly irresistible and his advice extraordinarily clear and easy to follow. For all explorers down the path of story, for all rebuilders of family and community, this is a highly recommended companion."

—Paula Underwood, executive director of The Past Is Prologue Education Program and author of *The Walking People* and *Who Speaks for Wolf*

"What a warm, moving, powerful book Richard Stone has written. It's filled with the beauty of human beings telling their stories. It's a rare find."

—Jay O'Callahan, professional storyteller

The Healing Art of Storytelling

Also by Richard Stone

Stories: The Family Legacy

T H E

Healing
Art

O F

Storytelling

A SACRED JOURNEY
OF PERSONAL DISCOVERY

Richard Stone

HYPERION

NEW YORK

Translation of "LIX—Last Night When I Was Asleep" by Antonio Machado on page 196, reprinted by permission of Maria M. Perez-Boudet.

Lines from "Folk Wisdom" by Thomas Kinsella on page 45 are reprinted by permission of the author.

Library of Congress Cataloging-in-Publication Data
Stone, Richard, 1951–
 The healing art of storytelling : using the power of story to
enrich your life / Richard Stone.—1st ed.
  p. cm.
 Includes bibliographical references (p.) and index.
 ISBN 0-7868-8107-0
 1. Storytelling—Religious aspects. 2. Stone, Richard, 1951– .
3. Spiritual life. I. Title.
 BL628.7.S76 1996
 808.5'43—dc20   96–376
                         CIP

Designed by Ann Gold

First Edition

10 9 8 7 6 5 4 3 2 1

ACKNOWLEDGMENTS

There are frequently rainmakers in our lives whose support and encouragement continually help us along the path. Louise Franklin Sheehy has been one such friend, and has championed my career every step along the way. Years ago, she urged me to develop a storytelling course for the Elderhostel program. It became the foundation for all of my subsequent work with families and hospices. Through her work with the Disney Institute, she suggested that Hyperion contact me to explore the idea of a book on storytelling and healing. I marvel at my good fortune and can only wonder, what next?

Many people have read early drafts of the book and made important contributions to its organization and the many ideas represented here. In the early going, Philip Golabuk helped me clarify my message and rethink the book's direction. My wife, Elizabeth, has continually been a sounding board for my ideas, and has lovingly reminded me over and over of the primacy of the body in any healing endeavor. In the last phases of editing, Kären Blumenthal and Ed Zogby were kind enough to read the manuscript and provide many insightful comments that shifted my thinking on a number of important issues.

I owe a special debt of gratitude to Laurie Chittenden, who has since left Hyperion. Without her initial interest and support of this project, it may never have made it through the many hurdles that any proposal must surmount. My special thanks go to my editor, Laurie Abkemeier, for her encouragement and continued faith in me and the book's message.

Last, I've had many teachers. All of the authors listed in Recommended Reading have helped to illuminate the way for me. But most of all, I owe a debt of gratitude to the many participants in my training programs who have been willing to share their stories and challenge my ideas.

CONTENTS

For days I have struggled with the task of beginning this book. The research has been complete for weeks. Ideas for each chapter were roughed out months ago. I could complain of writer's block, or the fact that there are so many things happening in my life that I haven't felt the physical and mental space to see clearly where to start. The truth is, until now there hasn't been a compelling reason to engage in the arduous task of writing. Even my editor's gentle prodding for the first few chapters did little to motivate me. Ironically, a relative's death has afforded me the time, the reflective space, and the desire to embark.

At this moment, I am flying at thirty thousand feet somewhere over the Gulf of Mexico on my way to my great-aunt's funeral in Los Angeles. When I heard of her passing last week, I knew that I had to be there. Not out of some vague obligation to her children and grandchildren, whom I see every decade or so. I needed to be there for me.

So much of my life seems to fly by into an abyss of insignificance, lacking distinction or real meaning. Many deaths in my family have gone that route, with work and personal obligations preventing me from attending the funerals. It's embarrassing to admit that weeks, and sometimes just days, later I have forgotten about their deaths, not to speak of the significance of their lives for me. I do not want this passing to be such a moment.

Even though I have rarely seen my aunt in the last thirty years, marking her death feels crucial to who I am. Some place in my soul knows that by being there I will come to appreciate her in new and important ways. In my memory, this woman was one of the few people in my childhood to unconditionally love me. I return to pay homage to her and discover, perhaps, something that is inexpressibly longing for connection within myself, calling out for healing.

As I see it, I'm on an archeological journey, searching for traces of my past, threads of understanding, and shards of memory that might help me construct a more panoramic picture of my life. The objects I seek are not clay and stone, though, but stories of my great-aunt Faye, her sister (my grandmother), my mother, and even me. These stories will hopefully reveal much more than the "facts" of my family—historical footnotes filled with dates and places. Maybe they will help me see more clearly the life forces and currents of meaning that preceded my entrance onto the scene. If I'm lucky, who I am will be richer, more complete, and expanded by the celebration of a long life that was well lived.

I dedicate this book to you, Aunt Faye, and thank you for your love, which still reaches across time to touch me deeply. Your death and my memories of all the ways you influenced my life have helped me to begin, reaffirming my work of showing others how the power of story can heal and repair our souls.

The Healing Art of
Storytelling

The Lay of the Land

Imagine mountains surrounded by old forests filled with pines and spruce that crawl up to jagged peaks. Unseen wildlife fill the woods with their calls and cries. Streams, running over large rocks, rush and bend out of sight. Multicolored lichen cover craggy tree trunks. The sun's light filters through the canopy overhead. Butterflies skate on the light breeze. Footprints of deer and bear, not more than a few hours old, stretch along the dirt path. Trails, crisscrossing this rich expanse, lead in every conceivable direction.

Having spent many solitary periods in the wilderness, I have come to appreciate a good topographical map when crossing rugged and beautiful terrain like this. Knowing the lay of the land really helps when planning a journey. With a reliable map you can discover the best trails and, if you're so inclined, areas accessible for bushwhacking—free-flow hiking beyond the neatly described and well-worn paths that have been traversed by others.

But a map is only a flat representation of what is, in truth, dynamic, changing, and full of the unexpected. There are many twists and turns not marked, and frequently the map can be of

1

little use when trail blazes are missing or an early winter storm creates a whiteout. In cases like these, you must follow your intuition, sometimes blindly heading into unknown and unexplored territory.

So it is with this book. My intention is that it will serve as a map into the territory we call experience and memory, showing you where I and others have traveled, and leading you into common areas of human experience that are so essential to this journey we call life. I expect that along the way you'll uncover lost and forgotten pieces of yourself that have been buried like valleys filled in by years of accumulating snow. And, in that process, perhaps you'll discover hidden places within your soul that are wellsprings of healing and life.

But, like all maps, this book can only point you in the right direction. You have to do the work by taking the first step. There are hundreds of trails to pursue, and you may find bushwhacking more to your taste. I encourage you to jump around, searching for the directions that speak to your current concerns and that appeal to your sense of wanderlust.

In whichever direction you turn, you will find that "story" is the homeward path. And, as in all explorations of a wilderness, you certainly will return to the trailhead a different person than the one who set out. Instead of the topo map you faithfully clung to when you began, the richness of all the mountains you struggled to climb and the streams you forded will become a reference point for what once was, abstractly, your past. These stories will serve you, guide you, fill you when you hunger for meaning, becoming a truer map for the journey ahead.

At the Trailhead

There are many paths to choose from at the trailhead. The world of social and political action can easily fill a lifetime. Or, we can follow in the footsteps of great humanitarians such as

Mother Teresa and Albert Schweitzer. I believe that before we can effectively repair the world, we must look inward, searching for wholeness among all the fractured parts. Thomas Moore suggests in *Care of the Soul* that there are four pathways for this inner-directed expedition: silence, song, dance, and storytelling.

Why did Moore attribute so much importance to a way of speaking and sharing that has all but gone out of fashion? Telling a story, especially about ourselves, may be one of the most personal and intimate things we can do. Through storytelling we can come to know who we are in new and unforeseen ways. We can also reveal to others what is deepest in our hearts, in the process, building bridges. The very act of sharing a story with another human being contradicts the extreme isolation that characterizes so many of our lives. As such, storytelling carries within it the seeds of community. And, because stories take time and patience, they serve as potent antidotes to a modern society's preoccupation with technology and speed.

When we recognize that our deepest aspirations cannot be satisfied by a culture that has reduced life's meaning to a smorgasbord of the senses and material possessions, we must search for new sources of meaning, struggling with the same questions that challenged our ancestors. Fortunately, they have left behind a trail, faintly marked at times, but there all the same. Their stories can lead us to a deeper understanding of our origins and where we are going. Paula Underwood, a close friend and author with Native American roots, calls this the "pathness" of life. Without a past, we have no place to stand, no promontory from which to see, no clear direction for our future actions.

Our longing to find our place in this world is more than just a feeling. Only when we stumble onto the "pathness" of our life do we come to understand that this feeling has been a beacon, not something to be avoided or snuffed out by absorption in the countless distractions around us. This became apparent to me a few years ago when I sent a student of mine to the library to discover the origins of his name. Lacking any real relationship with his father, he had no knowledge of his family's past, who his ancestors were or where he came from. He was bereft of stories. Sadly, he also seemed depressed. But, in the next class, he could hardly contain his excitement. Not only had he discovered where his clan had come from in Scotland, he had learned that the history of his first name was long and rich. He now had a story that he could call his own. A gaping hole in his being had been filled by a sense of belonging. You could see it in his face. There was life. Story can do that.

It's our nature to tell stories and to collect them. In fact, it's hard to conceive of life without story. After a hard day compounded by fighting traffic, one of the first things we do is tell our spouse or a friend about everything that happened—how the jerk in the yellow Camaro cut us off, nearly causing an accident, and how our employer just instituted a new policy at work for vacation time so that all the days we've been accumulating for an anticipated vacation are gone. This is not just passing the time of day. It's the mechanism through which we explain our world and come to understand who we are.

Story becomes the vehicle through which we organize the things that happen to us. It's also our way of telling time. Our life's story takes shape like chapters in a book, each in its proper place, one following the next, explaining why things were as they were, lending logic to our decisions and bringing meaning to what might otherwise be a collection of unrelated events. Without stories, life becomes a book cover without the pages—nice to look at, but not very fulfilling.

At the end of our lives, after we have passed on, all that is left of us is our story. In a peculiar way, these stories are our ticket to immortality. Knowing that future generations will retell our stories liberates us into a realm of timelessness.

Telling personal stories is also a bequest, a deeply meaningful and intimate legacy. Unfortunately, we sometimes fail to recognize these heartfelt gifts and listen with only one ear. When grandma tells us for the fortieth time how she came over to

America, we must see this tale as more than just the idle rambling of an old person with a failing memory. She's attempting to keep alive this recollection of her past because without it she is nothing. These are the pages in the book that are hers and hers alone.

Some years ago, when I was teaching an Elderhostel course, a participant approached me following the class. She wanted some advice. Her husband had died six months before, leaving explicit directions in his will that she spend $3,000 to publish his life story. She was angry and confused by his request that she waste money on something so inconsequential. Who would want to read the idle chatter of an old man whose life had been so ordinary? She wasn't even certain that her children would be interested. It wasn't a great piece of literature, and was only fifty pages long. "Why would he do such a thing?" she asked.

After spending three days in the course discovering and sharing her own life story, she had her answer. Standing before the class with tears in her eyes, she spoke of her love for her husband, and how he had loved her and their daughters. She also told the class the story of his life, his bequest, and how over the last four days her anger had been transformed into gratitude. By finally accepting the gift of his story and sharing it with others, she granted him not only his wish, but also a form of immortality. Who would have thought there was something so powerful in a simple tale waiting to be told?

PART ONE

Preparing for the Journey

CHAPTER 1

The Destorification of Our Lives

Why do we need a book to guide us on the inward journey that is accepted and commonplace in more traditional societies? Those of us who have visited other lands know that there is something frightfully wrong with the territory we call home. To make matters worse, what's missing can't be uncovered easily in our neck of the woods, regardless of how arduously we search. Most of the essential ingredients needed to support the story-telling journey have been lost along the way, and what's left can barely take root in the domain that we call postindustrial culture.

An Aerial View

Just as clear-cutting an old-growth forest leads to a phenomenon called deforestation—the stripping of the landscape of more than just trees—our culture has been devastated by the loss of storytelling as a tool for communicating, passing on values, learning, and, most important, healing. I call it *destorification*. Its effect is as devastating as its ecological cousin's. When you cut down the trees, you also destroy the multitude of microenvironments in which a host of other living creatures make their homes. Without the rich variety of trees, life cannot be sustained. Sadly, replanting as we practice it in this country does not re-create a forest. Row after row of tall pines do not entice the rich web of life to return. So it is with destorification. When social and economic pressures led to the disintegration of the intergenerational family, and, more recently, the breakdown of the nuclear family, something much deeper than a way of life died. In fact, the landscape in this country has changed so much that it's questionable as to whether storytelling, which has played an integral role until the twentieth century in every culture in the history of humankind, can take root and flourish once again.

There is so much that mitigates against the resurgence of storytelling. We live in a world addicted to speed and the bottom line. Few of us have the patience to listen to stories, much less explore their deeper relevance for our spiritual and emotional well-being. Many of us experience profound feelings of alienation, isolation, pain, and suffering while living solitary lives that seem to have no meaning. Evidence for this surrounds us: Teen suicide is reaching epidemic proportions; drug and alcohol addiction is destroying the foundation of our communities; the problems of racism and poverty seem to be flourishing at a time when this country's gross national product has never been greater; divorce is an expectation, not an exception; ethical and moral standards are sliding down a precipitous incline that seems to have no end; meaningful rituals that celebrate life appear to be lost even to the priests, ministers, and rabbis who are traditionally the keepers of our faiths; and yesterday's heroes and heroines are likely to appear on the front page of today's newspapers accused of immoral, unethical, and even criminal behavior. The litany of telltale signs that our social structures are decaying could intimidate even a wild-eyed optimist.

Searching for Bears, Ants, Coyotes, and Other Friendly Guides

None of us can live in this world and not experience and be wounded by painful losses. But some wounds are more subtle, going practically unnoticed. One in particular has been so buried beneath scar tissue that we live as though it had never occurred. But it's there, showing up daily in our speech under the guise of phrases like "out of sync," "out of touch," "I feel a little off today," and "I've got the blues." Sound familiar? These are expressions we all mutter from time to time when we're not quite with it, feeling as if our bodies and minds are not up to meeting the demands of the world. Headaches, allergies, and elevated blood pressure are just a few of the symptoms that tangibly express what may be a deeper issue that tears at our spiritual fabric.

These bodily manifestations have a wider significance, pointing to our culture's arrhythmia with the natural world. Whereas most generations who lived in preindustrial societies adapted themselves to organic rhythms, setting internal clocks to dawn and dusk, we have constructed an artificial time that has little or nothing to do with the animal and biological world in which we live. This change is far-reaching, affecting every detail of our lives.

Johnny Moses, a Native American storyteller, captures the importance of this issue in an ancient tale about the ebb and flow of day and night. In this story, Bear tries to enlist all the animals to accept a calendar in which the sun shines all day for six consecutive months and rests for the other six, leaving half the year in complete darkness. When Ant hears of this plan, she objects and challenges Bear to a dance. If Bear outlasts her, then there will be six months of daylight followed by six months of darkness, a real boon for Bear, who loves to sleep. If Ant succeeds, then the sun will rise and fall each day. Luckily for us, Ant triumphed when Bear fell sound asleep, exhausted by Ant's frenetic energy.

This story holds many important lessons for us. When we attempt to live outside the rhythms of nature and the animal kingdom, we not only exhaust ourselves by the effort, we also lose our connection to an important wellspring of energy and illumination. It's this link to other creatures that has often served as a bridge to understanding our own character. Stories about Coyote, Raven, Turtle, Hare, and, of course, Bear and Ant help us to see our own foibles as well as our own nobility. Each of us knows people who are bears through and through, preferring sleep over anything else. And the ants in our lives are an inspiration for all they can accomplish, as well as a nuisance for their incessant activity.

In this way, our world and all its living things become perfect reflections of who we are. Moreover, this system for categorizing personalities is descriptive and inherently accessible. While contemporary psychological tools are sophisticated, relying on complicated constructs such as ego, will, subconscious, introvert, and Type A, I'm not certain that they do more to elucidate our conspicuous and sometimes subtle stylistic differences. Phrases like "stubborn as a mule" or "quiet as a church mouse" tell us in very direct terms what a personality profile can only intimate. But it's not surprising that a culture disconnected from the land has resorted to a language that is depersonalizing and abstract.

In tribal societies, day and night each had a place in the framework of communal life. The tasks of survival were relegated to the hours during which the sun ruled. During the moon's watch, people assembled in circles around a central fire. There were important reasons for coming together—cooking, celebrating, singing, dancing, praying and other spiritual rituals. As the nights grew longer, storytelling often took the main stage. The central fire's radiance did more than warm the bones of those gathered there. Its flames fueled their imaginations, and, in a powerful way, provided a setting for weaving a group of people together. Fires of old melted the jagged edges of individuality, making it possible for a clan to create and sustain a community and a culture.

With inventions such as lanterns and electricity, we learned how to extend the day, disrupting the essential rituals of the night. While other creatures settle in at sunset, we continue to work, often alone, finding more and more reasons for not joining together around a central fire. Darkness, which fed the spirit of story, has been replaced by light. The loss of story has depleted our culture of time-honored heroes and wisdom, robbing us of our deep connection to our ancestors and ancient guiding myths.

Soapbox Substitutes

We no longer gather near a central fire. The bright lights we now assemble around are different than the roaring blazes of another age. They're television sets and computer screens carrying two-dimensional images and stories that do little to weave us together as a people. Through these media, cherished values and beliefs are relegated to insignificance, replaced by tales of greed and lust, sound bites and canned laughter, and commercial promises of a better life. Whereas storytelling fosters a spirit of community, television, video, computers, and even going to the movies produce the opposite effect.

Individuality and private experience are elevated to a stage of ultimate importance, leaving sparse spaces for togetherness. In today's world, it's not unusual for an entire family to subsist under one roof hardly knowing each other. A television in every bedroom now gives us the ultimate freedom to privately design and construct our own solitary world of entertainment. Community, if it exists, is relegated to sterile settings such as virtual reality and talk rooms on the Internet. Real intimacy has become scarce, surfacing in today's culture as sexualized fantasies and twisted notions of love and companionship.

These modern boxes of light also do little to illuminate our path or guide us along it. Even worse, they rob us of a personal and deep-rooted place where we might learn who we are, what we are, and where we have come from. In most traditional cultures, such lessons can be imparted only by the whole village, and especially by the elders, the keepers of these tales and the old ways. In our world, we have failed to create places of distinction for our matriarchs and patriarchs. We segregate and warehouse them, depriving the young of their wisdom and divesting them of the opportunity to make a valuable contribution. Ironically, the degree to which we are plugged in to all of the sources of information at our disposal seems to have an inverse relationship to our connectedness to ourselves, to others, and to a sense of personal history. We have become a culture obsessed with instant gratification and building a future without regard for our past, and we are in trouble.

Technological and entertainment wonders have become like religious shrines, occupying coveted positions in our homes, and are accepted without question as a progressive sign of our modernity. Like parasites, they slowly deplete our lives, leaving nothing substantial in return, only phantasms of what is real and important. In his book *In the Absence of the Sacred: The Failure of Technology and the Survival of the Indian Nations*, Jerry Mander, a courageous voice speaking out against the destructive nature of television, tells of the struggle of the Déné and Inuit tribes to resist the allure of television. Cut off from what we call civilization, these people still follow their ancient customs. But pressure by Canada's central government persuaded many of these isolated communities on the tundra to install satellite dishes and wire all their homes for TV. The subsequent tragedy that Mander describes took place swiftly.

Overnight, he witnessed the death of all that was important and sacred. Elders who were the revered guardians of their community's history and traditional stories, and thereby the transmitters of values and ethics, ceased their telling. Time that would customarily have been devoted to caring for their grandchildren was consumed with watching TV, fourteen to sixteen hours a day. Cherished crafts vanished, victims of game shows, talk shows, and sitcoms. Behavior problems in schools suddenly rose to epidemic proportions. The substance of ancient lore passed down by the ancestors was replaced by neatly packaged pabulum in the form of afternoon soap operas.

The culture's final curtain was noticed by few. Even fewer cared. The reality of genuine community was replaced by the surreal specter of elders praying for the lives of the poor souls who star in made-for-TV melodramas.

Native peoples are quickly losing a connection to their rich past, and are losing themselves in the process. Unfortunately, we are no different. Only, the death occurred some decades ago. Blindly, we live within a culture that is adrift and unsustaining.

Nobody's Home

We have become like shadows in the world, depleted from within. The area in which it's most apparent is in the shrinking ability of adults and children to use their imaginations. Teachers tell me that they have witnessed a steady decrease in elementary students' verbal and artistic ability during the last fifteen years. When asked to write an original story, kids today are much more likely to regurgitate the plot from the latest movie thriller with a cast of pop characters from Saturday morning cartoons. Gone is the ability to make up a story out of nothing.

We adults are in far worse shape. Neighbors marching off to work in starched shirts and blue suits are easily identifiable victims of imperiled imagination. Regardless of the outward manifestations, though, each of us is to one degree or another a casualty of a culture that devalues what I consider to be the most important ingredient of human sanity: imagination. Just as an individual who is deprived of dream time becomes psychotic, a person robbed of imagination time during waking hours becomes psychically and spiritually numb. Unfortunately, the mass culture serves up television and other recreational fillers to distract both adults and children from encountering this rich inner life. The consequences are far-reaching, affecting much more than educational and aesthetic issues. Mander suggests that our disjunction from imagination can also be concealed under the guise of addictive behavior.

In the days before satellite dishes and cable, creative play was the norm. When we got home from school, we'd go through what Mander calls "downtime," unwinding from the compression of a day filled with classes and learning. I remember getting a snack from the refrigerator, lying on the couch, and relishing the fact that I was doing absolutely nothing. It wouldn't take too long, though, before boredom took over. After a while I'd either be nudging my mom because there was "nothing to do," in which case she would kick me out of the house to play, or I'd go into my room and devise my own play by reading, drawing, or building something. Within a few minutes, I'd be totally absorbed in a game of kick the can with my friends, or building a model battleship. Without boredom I never would have been motivated to get up and do something creative.

Today, this scenario looks very different. When a kid comes home, he grabs a snack and heads for the TV room. Before he can experience "downtime" and the discomfort of boredom, he turns the TV on and begins surfing the channels. In fact, the TV is used to relieve and mask these restless feelings. The result is that children today use TV as a mood-altering experience, much like adults use alcohol and drugs. Mander paints a frightening picture—television as the training ground for future addiction.

As the winds of our changing society buffet and blow us into what many feel is a despairing future, what can we do to create a world that nurtures our souls and feeds our imaginations? How do we forge a new path that can heal us and bind us together?

To Begin Again

Repairing the damage is a daunting task, but one that calls out to us, prompting our deepest sensibilities to undertake the journey. In searching for a model of how to start, I have found wisdom in one of the oldest stories in Western civilization—the tale of the expulsion of Adam and Eve from the Garden of Eden. In the rabbinic commentaries on this story, we find two people who are devastated by their loss. Everything is gone—their home, eternal life, a world free of toil and pain, beauty beyond anything imaginable, and the unconditional love and affection of their Creator. Unlike those of us whose transgressions are many, their downfall can be attributed to just one indiscretion. But, like us, they found themselves cast out, strangers in the world, everything meaningful left behind. They were the first pilgrims, wandering the world with nothing but the clothes on their backs, searching for a place to call home. For many, this would be a cause for despair. The best of us would wallow in our own self-pity. Where would we find the courage and strength to re-create our world, to fashion a new order?

In this story, though, are the seeds for personal and cultural renewal. In his book *Messengers of God: Biblical Portraits and Legends*, Elie Wiesel teaches us that Adam and Eve's most important legacy is a simple but powerful medicine with remarkable curative powers for today's challenges—in spite of everything, Adam and Eve chose to begin again. We, too, must find the courage and will to repair our world. How do we begin again?

First, we must consciously choose the mystique of the night over the realities of daylight and work, rediscovering in the process our own rhythms, which are rooted in our biological and

cultural heritage. We must also say no to television and the unlimited media spin-offs that are alluring but for the most part
lacking in emotional and spiritual substance. Then, we must affirm storytelling, reinstating it as a central motif in the framework of our lives.

CHAPTER 2

The Body and Soul of Storytelling

How does story work its magic, forging community where only moments before there was none? Why do we humans love a good story, capable of being transformed and transported by the drama of someone else's life?

The mechanism for these miracles is remarkably simple. If we could open up the mind like the hood of a car, we'd find the answer in our wiring. While experience is encoded by all the senses, the primary fuel that ignites our memory is pictorial. Yes, there are exceptions. Many of us rely on other senses for our principal knowledge of our world. But, regardless of a person's learning orientation, I have consistently found that for most of us who are sighted, it's the *images* of past events that are most accessible to recollection.

The Key to Remembrance

Like a movie, memories are strung together in scenes that segue one into the next. Sometimes these transitions are slow fades, with pictures flowing seamlessly into one other. Often they are arranged in a sequence of staccato stills, abruptly colliding with remembrances that seem distantly, if at all, related. Unlike a permanent medium such as videotape, which permits us to replay the same images over and over, never varying no matter how many times we rewind the tape, replaying memories reveals a medium that is much more fluid and pliant.

Each time we journey inward and trace the path of a memory to its origins, we seem to discover nuances and connections that previously went unnoticed. The illumination of our current awareness is conditioned by our emotional state and by seemingly inconsequential matters such as the aroma of a pie baking or the sound of a passing train, thereby filtering the process of recollection in the way light is filtered through a prism.

For example, the subtle touch of a friend's hand on my shoulder can open a door to a whole realm of past experience that I haven't considered for forty years. Suddenly I see myself standing in front of our old house, my mother's arms wrapped around me. An old girlfriend's beautiful, shining face intrudes on this memory, and I wait for her caress, which never materializes. Her still hand metamorphoses into my grandfather Morris's rough, burly hand, with fingers the size of Polish sausages. My mind roams through a multitude of images of Morris, and warm feelings wash over me. In that instant, my friend increases the pressure of her hand on my shoulder. I turn. Her warm face welcomes me. She asks if I'm ready to go. I nod as I rise, gathering my things.

In the space of no more than a second or two, all these scenes flashed by, barely noticed, abruptly drowned out by the matters at hand, and just as quickly forgotten. Rarely do we recognize how awareness of the past flows into the present, and how the present ebbs back into the past. Memories fly by like a high-speed train, a subtle undercurrent to sensory experience. It's as though the senses assert an intoxicating effect on our consciousness, keeping the past enshrouded in a murky light.

If we allow ourselves to be drawn inward, purposefully cast-

ing the light of awareness in that direction, something remarkable happens. Our past merges with the present, allowing us to
reclaim and re-create a hidden domain. But moving against the
tide of the present requires a conscious decision, an act of will
to remember. As simple as such a decision may seem, there is
something profoundly sacred in reclaiming the past.

In *The Spirituality of Imperfection*, Ernest Kurtz and Katherine
Ketcham beautifully illustrate the sanctity of stories with an
anecdote about the Baal Shem Tov, the founder of Jewish Cha-
sidism. His disciples cautiously asked him why he always answered a question with a story. They steeled themselves, expecting that he would answer this question with a story as well.
Thoughtfully, the Baal Shem Tov replied, "I answer your questions with stories because salvation lies in remembrance." The
will to remember may be the first and most important step on
the healing path.

Time

What is the past? Is there a biological equivalent to a camcorder
somewhere in our brains that makes an unmistakable record of
everything that has occurred? Can we ever get to the *truth* of what
happened? How is it that two people can grow up in the same
home and have radically divergent views of their family's history?
Is one right and the other wrong?

Time is organic, malleable, and unfixed. What we call "the
past" is not just a compilation of historical facts such as marriages, illnesses, births, and deaths—although these events certainly play a significant role in creating the person each of us has
become. In truth, how we describe the past is much more a
function of our current concerns, issues, perspectives, and intentions. And our description is really all that we have. There is
no final authority to confirm our views.

The future—as expressed in our hopes and dreams and

plans—also can affect how we portray the past. For example, if as a child you always wanted to travel to the South Seas, read everything there was on the subject, but never had an opportunity to make the trip, you might look back on this dream as one of the biggest disappointments of your life. It may even be a source of pain and discouragement that bleeds over into a description of other areas of your childhood, such as a belief that might sound like, "My parents never encouraged me and criticized everything I ever wanted to try."

One day, though, an uncle dies and leaves you some money, just enough to make this journey. When you arrive in Tahiti, it turns out to be different from what you imagined. Not so romantic. Certainly not as ideal as you had pictured it as a child. In fact, the experience falls so short of your expectations that it fundamentally alters the way you see your childhood. Whereas before you might have thought harshly of your mother, who always criticized your notion of traveling to faraway places, you now understand her better. She unexpectedly appears wise, even a stabilizing influence in your young world filled with fantasies that needed grounding. This is in stark contradiction to your assessment of her as you were growing up. You can no longer tell the same story as before. Your past has been changed, in a sense, by the future. And it may be changed again by other travels and discoveries.

Sounds strange, doesn't it? Even illogical. That's because time is filled with its own quirky uncommon sense, resistant to the meter of grandfather clocks measuring each moment in exact proportions, one after the other.

Viewing the past is like peering through a stained-glass window from dawn to dusk. As the sun moves across the sky, the illumination of the many facets of glass changes. As I walk about the room, intricate patterns that were hidden in darkness reveal themselves only from certain angles. From afar, the window may seem like an expanse of muted ochres and browns. Up close, complementary veins of red, green, orange, and blue stand out with brilliant clarity and distinction.

At its heart, what we call *experience* is an interpretative, not a perceptive, encounter. Seeing is one thing. But how we choose to interpret what we see will determine the story we tell and the life we lead. That's how two people can witness the same event but tell two entirely different stories about what each saw.

As an interpretation, the past can be reinterpreted at any moment. If there is such a thing as freedom, this may be it. No longer must we be a victim of the stories we tell about our past, forever suffering the emotional and physical pain associated with disturbing childhood events. We can become both a character in our play as well as its author.

What Our Bodies Know

Our stories are not only mental narratives that engage our imagination, or a string of interesting and meaningful pictures, ideas, and dialogue. Rather, story has the power to go right through us, reaching into every cell, changing our chemistry, and profoundly affecting our well-being. How can something that has been relegated to the province of children be so powerful?

There is a saying that goes, "The body does not know the difference between an imagined event and a real one." Likewise, the body does not distinguish between real events and those that are represented in story form. Test it for yourself. Sit comfortably. Imagine that you are standing at street level before a large skyscraper. See yourself walking through the lobby doors and entering an elevator, pushing the button for the forty-third floor. When the elevator arrives and the doors open, exit to your right. You see a metal door leading out onto a balcony. Push it open and step outside. You discover that this is a construction site. The walls and railings of the balcony have been removed. Carefully, walk to the concrete edge and peer over it at the traffic forty-three stories below you. Nothing but air separates you and the pavement. One slip and . . .

If you are feeling anxious about the prospect of venturing this close to danger, you have probably already terminated this fantasy, returning your attention to the present and to your comfortable surroundings. Isn't it remarkable that just the thought of something that scary can produce all the discomfort that would accompany the real thing? As far as your body was concerned, you *were* on the forty-third floor and you *were* in danger of falling.

The inverse is also true. Stories that are filled with positive, healing images can create a physiological state that biochemists would associate with health, relaxation, and emotional well-being. Research bears this out.

Traditional cultures are way ahead of this scientific curve, though, having used story as a powerful adjunct to healing for millennia. For example, in some Islamic societies you would never bring a sick person flowers and candies as we do in this country. Instead, you would tell them a story of patience, endurance, and triumph. The images such a tale would plant in their awareness would circulate through their souls just as powerfully as a medicinal elixir would travel to the diseased cells by way of the bloodstream. The more the story is considered, the more it can empower the body's own healing mechanisms.

In Hindu medicine, fairy tales are used metaphorically to effect changes in persons suffering from mental afflictions. It is hoped that by contemplating the tale, the sufferer may find a path through and beyond the emotional disturbance. Hindu physicians understand that a story can work upon the psyche in mysterious and incomprehensible ways. The tale functions as a koan, a guide, a model, and a teacher to the listener, transforming a stuck mental process into one that flows like a story does from a beginning to a conclusion. If the protagonist in the story can find peace and tranquility at the end of the proverbial rainbow, there is hope for all who listen who have lost themselves along the way.

Unfortunately, in our society we lack a collection of such stories in both personal and collective memory. Even if we had the stories at our command, few of us would recognize their importance. If by chance we understood their significance, even fewer would know how to share them. We have no history of respecting the subtle power of the tale and must learn again how to relish stories, much the way we might learn to appreciate a fine cognac that must be sipped, savored, and slowly ingested.

Hospital settings and other healthcare environments must be totally reassessed, making room for institutional models of healing that incorporate storytelling and other art forms such as dance and song. How odd this suggestion may seem in light of currently respected practices, but even traditionalists are opening themselves to the possibility that the quickest route to healing the body is through the psyche and the soul. Like shamans in tribal societies, storytellers may soon be walking the halls of hallowed medical institutions dispensing their remedies one tale at a time.

CHAPTER 3

Transformative Stories

In a world in which we privatize everything, including personal experience, story may be the one thread that can connect us to more expansive realities. The internal realm represented by pseudonyms such as "unconscious" and "transcendent Self" rarely reveals itself directly to us, preferring to be shrouded in a curtain of dreams and metaphors. Ironically, when we share our stories and hear life tales from others, we stumble upon this luminous underworld in unpredictable ways. In my life, through the creation of stories, unresolved conflicts and needs have unexpectedly appeared, and, in the process, worked themselves out.

Unexpected Destinations

A few years ago, this phenomenon dramatically revealed itself when a member of the local storytellers' guild asked me to create a story for a special Christmas performance. It seemed a simple enough request. Little did I know that this would be an opportunity to transform my relationship with my father. Being

Jewish, I thought hard about my experiences of Chanukah, looking for some kernel that could be expanded into a full-blown
tale. What I discovered was that my experience of Chanukah was
inextricably intertwined with the event of Christmas. I couldn't
talk about one without the other. And I couldn't think about
Christmas without remembering my best friend's father and his
love affair with this holiday, which led me to my own father.

Most of my life I felt that my relationship with my dad had
been lacking. He was always working too hard to give me the
attention I craved. After a while, I stopped asking, neatly stor-
ing away the hurt and the loss. But these things don't go away.
This particular Christmas season they resurfaced, auguring a new
relationship with him. Here's the story:

CHRISTMAS ON TERRACE DRIVE

Christmas in my neighborhood was always heralded on a warm
Florida day by the reenactment of the divine birth of the baby
Jesus right in Paul McCloskey's front yard. Paul was my best
friend, and his dad, a doctor, constructed this scene out of
beautifully painted plywood—a manger and three wise men
with a host of animals watching Mary and Joseph as they adored
the Christ child. An electric star suspended from a tree glowed
above them, and Saint Nick was there with his team of reindeer
coming in for a three-point landing. I always imagined that he
wanted to take a peek, too. A beatific angel resting on the roof
looked on with joyous approval. Colored lights were strung
everywhere, blinking like tiny beacons in the night. It was all
part of Christmas on Terrace Drive, and people came for miles
to gaze at the good doctor's masterful creation.

During the off-season, all the players in this heavenly drama
rested in the rafters of the McCloskey garage. To visit Paul, I
had to go through there to get to the back door. I often paused
to look at the Virgin Mary as she stared down at me, smiling
peacefully. Her gaze was almost like the Mona Lisa's, following
me wherever I walked. Unfortunately, moments like these were
frequently interrupted when a large palmetto bug—many of

which lived in the garage—scurried across her shoulder, disappearing into the motley assemblage of junk stored overhead.

The yearly unveiling took shape the weekend following Thanksgiving. Early Saturday, Paul helped his dad dust off the leading characters in the Christmas play. I always went by to observe and, invariably, help. Dr. McCloskey stood on a stepladder with a filterless Camel hanging from his lip and a mesh T-shirt clinging to his sweaty chest. The humidity was high, and the garage temperature was always twenty degrees hotter than the day's official reading. Paul's dad grunted and mumbled instructions between his teeth as the ash on his cigarette grew. I waited, hoping to see it hit Paul in the head.

Carefully, Dr. McCloskey passed the cut plywood figures down to Paul's waiting hands. They were too heavy for Paul to manage. After Joseph slipped from his grip and crashed face first on the oily garage floor, Dr. McCloskey's short Irish fuse blew and he cursed up and down. Then he looked at me, yelling, "Don't just stand there like a bump on a log. Get over here and lend a hand, son!"

There I was, a good Jewish boy, cradling the baby Jesus, Mary, and the little lambs, partaking in my own way in the sacrament of Christmas. We carried each of the figures to the front yard, between the two giant holly trees. When they had all been hauled out, we hammered stakes into the ground and bolted each into place. But this was only the beginning.

There were the spotlights to contend with and giant ornaments the size of a human head. Then we had to retrieve two large boxes stored in the most remote corner of the garage. Inside were what seemed like miles of electric wire and bulbs. No matter how much care was taken the previous year, they were always hopelessly tangled. This mess left Dr. McCloskey grumbling, complaining, and blaming Paul for the puzzle, which took an hour to unravel. "Have you boys been fooling with these lights?"

"No, sir!" Paul responded, his Irish temper also beginning to flare in the face of his father's accusations. I just shook my head, hoping to stay out of the cross fire.

It was nearly one in the afternoon by the time we plugged them in for a test, and we still hadn't eaten lunch. One string of lights had a loose plug and didn't work at all, and many of the bulbs on the others needed replacing.

"Damn!" Dr. McCloskey said as he marched off to get his wallet. We were all tired and hungry and ready for a break. "Come on boys," he said, returning less irritated. "I'll buy you a burger at the Old Meeting House. Then we'll stop by the hardware store for bulbs."

By the time the shakes and fries were served, he was smiling and joking. "Yep, I think it's going to look real good this year." To me, it was going to look the way it looked every year, but for Dr. McCloskey it was as though he were putting it up for the first time.

An hour later, he precariously balanced on the edge of the roof as he tacked the lights to the front of the house. Paul stood on the ladder feeding him the wire. I scurried between the box and the ladder doing the same for Paul. Both of us wanted to be up on the roof as well, but his dad reminded us that we were still too young for such dangerous work. Paul asked if we'd be old enough next year. "Yeah, maybe," said Dr. McCloskey. "We'll talk about it. Now hand me some more wire." He had been saying this for years now. The truth is, he never let us up on the roof, even when we were plenty old enough. Dr. Mc-Closkey was in his element as he towered above us looking out over the neighborhood.

By four-thirty we were ready to put the final touches on the masterpiece, carefully suspending the ornaments from the tree branches. This was a job for Paul and me. Like monkeys, we scurried up the ladder and crawled out on limbs that would never have supported Dr. McCloskey. From below he yelled instructions. "Over a little . . . to the next branch . . . Paul, can't you listen to me? . . . now, not quite so low . . . careful, it's going to fall. . . ."

Sure enough, without fail, Paul dropped at least one of those ornaments every year. Sometimes, a miracle occurred that seemed more incredible to me than the virgin birth. It hit the ground, bounced two or three times in the grass, then came to rest, unbroken. More often than not, it shattered into three or four huge pieces. Dr. McCloskey silently shook his head while glaring at Paul and fuming. "Goddammit, do you know how much these things cost? What does it take for you to watch what you're doing?" His voice trailed off as Paul winced.

When the job was completed and Paul had leaped to the ground from the lowest limb, Dr. McCloskey directed us to go stand across the street in front of my house and watch as he flipped the switch. By this time it was dusk, and the last glimmers of daylight were disappearing in an outburst of red and orange in the western sky. When the colored spots illuminating the manger and Saint Nick flicked on, Paul and I clapped and screamed at the top of our lungs. Then the lights adorning the house and the bushes popped on, and we grew silent. Dr. McCloskey walked backward from the front porch and stepped across the curb, hardly watching where he was going. As he joined us, something magical happened. He put one hand on Paul's shoulder, the other on mine, and gave a gentle squeeze. That feeling of accomplishment, then recognition, was something I had hardly ever known with my dad. All the scurrying around and attempts to please this cantankerous man had been worth it. He repaid me a thousand times over with that one squeeze of his hand.

Because of Dr. McCloskey, Christmas had become something glorious and mystical, much more than a religious event. Childishly, I thought that perhaps if we had a Christmas tree that spirit could enter my home, too.

Convincing my parents wasn't such a difficult task. My father, an avowed agnostic and rationalist, could not object on religious grounds. For him, it was an understandable request given that all my friends had one. He was surprisingly sympathetic.

My mother had to be won over by the oldest childhood ploy—badger them until they can't take it anymore, then turn the screws and whine. She hated the thought of a "Chanukah bush" inside our home. Whatever we called it, it was still a Christmas tree. Bringing such a symbol into the heart of our living room no doubt offended her deepest religious sensibilities, but not nearly as much as my nagging gnawed on her nerves.

One week before Christmas, she consented to take me to Richard's Drugstore and buy an artificial tree, tinsel, decorations, and our own string of lights. When everything was in place, I plugged in the cord and stood back, nearly as pleased at that moment as when Paul, his dad, and I stared at our creation, stretching from one end of their yard to the other. That night, I fell asleep on the floor watching the blinking lights as they reflected off the glass bulbs. The more I struggled to keep my eyes open, the more kaleidoscopic the lights became.

The next day, I invited Paul, Jody, and Eddie to come see my tree. Now I was one of them, a member of the club. They said it was nice, although it hardly compared with the live eight-footers that graced their living rooms.

Looking down on the McCloskeys' glorious tribute to Christmas on one side of the street, and the sacrilegious display of an artificial Christmas inside the house across from theirs, God must have had quite a chuckle. I guess that's why He arranged for Rabbi Zielonka to call my mom the Sunday before Christmas. The rabbi wanted to visit us that afternoon! Rabbi Zielonka had never stopped by our house, and his choosing this particular weekend was a bad omen. My mother panicked after she hung up the receiver. My father, always displaying steadiness in the face of adversity, also seemed a little worried. What we needed was a plan. "We'll just move everything into Ricky's room, close the door, and what the rabbi doesn't know won't hurt him," he said. My mother reluctantly agreed, but kept mumbling that it was my father's fault we were in this mess in the first place.

"I think God's punishing us," she said half seriously. My father smirked and shook his head. He was in control of the situation, not God. Everything would work out fine. Privately, I wondered if my mother might be right.

When Rabbi Zielonka arrived, our house appeared to be cleansed from the scourge of Christmas. The menace, though, lurked quietly next to my bed.

We gathered in the living room, where my mom served coffee and Danishes. While she was busy pouring and acting as the perfect hostess, the rabbi took a special interest in me. He wanted to know everything I was doing, thinking, and learning. At the time, the most important thing in my life was making a replica of a World War II destroyer. It was almost three feet long, and I described to him in precise detail the gun turrets and the small canisters that were depth charges for destroying enemy subs.

"You know, I served on a ship much like that during the war. I'd love to see it," he said, getting out of his chair. "It's in your room?"

In what felt like slow motion, both my parents looked at me with alarm shooting like arrows from their eyes. I think my heart stopped beating. By this time the rabbi was standing, waiting for me to lead the way to certain doom. I leaped to my feet and bounded out of the living room before he moved another step. "I'll bring it to you," I yelled, now halfway down the hall.

I slid the door open and shut it behind me, leaning up against its cold, hard surface, realizing that I had just averted an eternal curse on my family. When I returned with the battleship and handed it to the rabbi for his praise and adoration, my parents' eyes silently showered me with their thanks. My mom returned to pouring coffee and serving the Danishes.

Uncharacteristically, my dad praised all the hard work I had put into that model. Then, he did something totally unexpected. He came over to where I stood, put his hand on my shoulder, and gave me a loving squeeze.

Looking back, I now realize that writing "Christmas on Terrace Drive" created a miracle in my life. In actuality, after age four or five I don't remember my father ever giving me that kind of physical praise and reassurance. But it's what I wanted from him more than anything else. Ironically, it's not clear whether he stopped giving or I stopped asking. I suspect it was a bit of both. One Saturday afternoon, I remember him sleeping on the living-room couch. I was standing there, silently, about a foot from his head, hoping he'd wake and play with me. My mother whispered to me to come in the other room, then admonished me for bothering him. "Can't you see how hard your dad works? He's tired. Leave him alone and go outside and play with your friends." Unfortunately, I took her words too seriously. Never again did I ask.

Most of the events in the story happened as I described them, but I chose to fashion an ending that contradicts the reality I unwittingly helped to create as a child. Just because I'm now an adult does not mean that I don't need a memory, or, at the least, an image of a father who was affectionate and attentive. This was the father I wanted. It's also the father I still need.

As I have told this story over and over through the last few years, it has reminded me of the fact that my dad *did* love me, even though at times he seemed distant. More important, it has given me a model for how I want to be with him *now*. Instead of accepting the perfunctory male slap on the back when we visit, I now give him a real hug and even a tight squeeze of the shoulder while telling him how much I love him. And, as I have invited him to share his life stories, I've discovered that he never had a dad who gave him a tight squeeze of the shoulder. He, too, was searching for reassurance and acknowledgment. Instead of living in a story of how little my dad was there for me, a new perspective has evolved—one that is filled with compassion, understanding, and appreciation. It's not surprising that our relationship has continued to grow. From my viewpoint, it's the best it has ever been. I was not expecting to get all that from a simple story about tinsel and Chanukah lights.

In my own life, I have seen storytelling bring together even enemies who are committed to each other's mutual destruction. A number of years ago, I participated in an organization called the Foundation for Mideast Communication. We were a loosely defined group with chapters in many of this nation's major cities as well as in Jerusalem. The foundation had one principal goal—to promote dialogue and understanding among the disparate groups who have a stake in the future of the Mideast. We felt that if there was to be any possibility for a lasting peace between the Arabs and the Jews, it had to start with one-to-one dialogue that transcended the rhetoric of distrust and hate.

Our primary vehicle for accomplishing this goal was a day-long communication workshop that encouraged participants to examine their cherished beliefs about each other and the long-standing conflict. The most important outcome of these sessions was that for the first time we had the opportunity to hear one another's stories: how we have been hurt by the antagonism between our communities and nations; our personal and collective losses; our anger, hatred, and desire for revenge; and our cherished aspirations for a different world, one not built on violence. Arabs heard for the first time the pain and hopes expressed in stories told by their sworn enemy. Jews were able to hear their own story mirrored in the lives of the Arabs who sat across from them.

We did not solve all of the Mideast's problems. I would like to think, though, that our work made a small contribution to what is now an active peace process. Most important, out of these experiences many of us forged friendships with people whom we once thought were less than human. What we discovered in our stories was our shared humanity and our mutual pain, thereby creating a community of caring that has endured over the last ten years. The foundation's work was a testimony to the power of storytelling to heal even the most invidious, gaping wounds that separate people.

Story can also build the fires of community in unexpected ways. In *The Spirituality of Imperfection*, Kurtz and Ketcham recount a brief anecdote that illustrates how complete strangers can be drawn into a web of closeness simply through the telling of a tale.

About noon one working day, an itinerant clown stood at the edge of New York City's Central Park, juggling and engaging the passersby by calling out questions, inviting them to sit down, making them laugh. Little by little a crowd gathered. After a while, a man in a three-piece suit looked at his watch and realized that he had to return to work. Moved by the performance, he went to drop a twenty-dollar bill into the hat at the clown's feet.

"Don't give me twenty dollars!" the clown called out. "Buy us some apples instead!"

The man in the three-piece suit was startled but receptive; within ten minutes he returned with a bag of apples for the group.

And with those apples a little community was created in Central Park—twenty people eating apples, watching a juggler. When others came by to watch, the only way the newcomers could be transformed from confused outsiders to members of the group would be if somebody told them "the story of the apples."

Story has the power to invite us into the growing circles gathered around community fires. Now it is up to us to build new fires and create new circles that are inclusive, welcoming strangers and world travelers into our lives, and our stories.

Many Paths, Many Circles

Remember the children's song that ends in the refrain, "Merrily, merrily, merrily, merrily, life is but a dream"? Tragically, we can go through an entire lifetime with no sense of the meaning of our suffering and pain, and without a context for understanding our joys and triumphs. It can seem like a dream with fifty, sixty, even seventy years feeling like a passing moment. How do we anchor ourselves, securing our worldly and private experiences so that they aren't just flotsam on the rivers of time?

Completion and fulfillment of a life well lived is bestowed only through translating our past into stories that are then externalized through speaking or writing. Until we share our life in this way, our experiences are just extraneous historical relics. Through a story, even seemingly insignificant details can hold remarkable importance to the meaning of our lives. Unfortunately, many of the elders I have taught denigrate their past. They'd rather not look back at an existence that may have been painful, impoverished, and meaningless. Coming to America was an escape from all of that. Why should they waste their time remembering?

When a person has decided that the past is a closed book, it's difficult to offer a compelling argument for taking a different tack. I can only report that those who choose to remember return with unexpected riches. As we grow older, this journey back in time appears to be increasingly important to living with a sense of fulfillment and completion. Some contemporary writers in the field of aging, such as Rabbi Zalman Schachter-Shalomi, even suggest that it's all part of the developmental process, as essential as crawling, walking, and leaving home. There's no way around it: A life "unstoried," regardless of its length, is, in an undeniable way, stunted.

We begin our worldly journey by accumulating a whole battery of experiences. When events occur, we may reach a conclusion about their meaning and relevance based on our current knowledge, understanding, and feelings, interpreting each as either a success or a failure, good or bad, pleasurable or painful. If we never revisit these conclusions, not only is our past frozen in time—a story with no room to breathe—our present and future may become extensions of this cold reality. We become stuck, lifeless, deadened, caught forever in an endless replay of old and often painful narratives. The real tragedy is that these scripts are so powerful, they can strangle the present, even constricting our life's physical energies.

But, when we undertake the task of making sense of our lives, searching for the maps that connect the many disparate paths we have traveled, we not only shed light on our pasts, we also complete a circle by connecting the past to our current concerns, feelings, needs, aspirations, and outlook. In this way we discover our truth, at least for now. Tomorrow, the entire landscape may be changed by a single event or recollection, giving us reason to reassess everything that we heretofore neatly analyzed, understood, and stored away for future consideration.

A number of years ago, while working with a group of adult children of alcoholics, I had an opportunity to witness this process in action. Most of these people had grown up in abusive households, with at least one parent recklessly out of control. For many, their stories about their alcoholic parents were fixed by images of drunkenness and violence. Worse yet, their assessments of their childhoods were reduced to a few frightening pictures of being victimized in a nightmarish play.

During my work with them, they participated in the "House Tour," an exercise that appears later in this book. When I asked them to draw the floor plans of the homes they had grown up in, many expressed reluctance and fear. As far as they were concerned, those places were *only* filled with pain and sorrow—the source of their many difficulties in current relationships. Why should they return home to relive these awful experiences?

What many discovered was startling, shaking their self-images to the core. Certainly, memories of abuse and pained relationships with fathers and mothers were stirred up. What also rose to the top of the pot were recollections of fond and pleasant times, long forgotten and discarded because they did not fit into their prevalent life narratives. Fathers who had been unidimensional drunks suddenly came to life, at times compassionate and caring, and truly present. Meals that had been disrupted by arguments were suddenly counterbalanced by harmonious holidays when, if only for brief moments, everyone was talking and sharing. There were even times of joy that had been neatly locked away in the craggy recesses of their memories.

These positive recollections were dissonant with the personal themes that had led them to seek help. Could it be that their stories were incomplete? That they would have to revise their current description of their past, and their parents? That, perhaps, they could create a new story of the past that would, in the present, be more empowering? Many of these people made new connections and told new stories. In doing so, they discovered a freedom that was not present in the previous accounts, which had been painted with a palette containing only shades of brown and gray. Where there had been stories of despair, there now existed tales that were softer, filled with characters that cried out for respect and understanding. These were also people from whom lessons could be learned, and whose lives, in part, could serve as a model for those they had victimized. And, where victims of a horrendous past once stood, there now stood human beings who had been wounded by some of the things that had happened in their childhoods. But these wounds were not fatal. They had become medals that could proudly be worn, evidence of triumph in the face of mortal danger. More important, by recovering these forgotten stories, these people had reclaimed their lives from tyrannical scripts that offered no hope for a better future. Only by making the journey back could they come full circle and be truly at home in the present.

Only Time Will Tell

The conclusions we live with frequently harm us in devastating ways. But conclusions can often show up in a more subtle and unrecognizable fashion. Declarations that the world was out to get us today, that an event was a terrible piece of bad luck, or that life would be fine if it weren't for someone else's actions are all symptoms of stories that can keep us stuck.

If you are like me, you carry around a template of how the world should be—what would make for a perfect day, a great year at work, successful relationships, and even a good life. So far, few of my expectations have been met. Just when things seem to be going fine, life throws me a curve and I'm left reeling, attempting to find a new footing on a playing field not of my design or choosing.

How I respond to these changes makes a world of difference to my sense of well-being. In essence, it all boils down to the story I adopt. If my car's engine starts spewing smoke on a trip, delaying my arrival by a day, I could spin a tale of victimization, blaming the mechanic for his incompetence and the manufacturer for shoddy workmanship. All these things may be true, but this firmly drawn conclusion to my story eliminates a whole world of opportunity. It also becomes an event that is incongruous with the rest of my life, irrelevant and meaningless to anything else going on. The more quickly I put it behind me, the better.

This happened to me once on the way to college. I was stuck overnight in White Springs, Florida, miles from anywhere, waiting for a part to arrive by bus. Never in a million years would I have stopped at this sleepy country town. But there I was with time on my hands, bemoaning my bad luck. As I look back, though, I realize that it was not all that bad. In fact, this breakdown was filled with adventure and learning. Did you know that the Suwannee River flows through this north Florida town and that, in recognition of his famous song, a memorial to Stephen Foster is built there? That Foster wrote that tune and composed the lyrics without ever seeing the river in person? Or, that there are countless intriguing and tragic legends about the Suwannee? Neither did I.

At that time, the story I told about this fateful excursion was filled with self-pity and the inconvenience of it all. But the way I see it now is that it was an event brimming with the joy of discovery. All of my other trips to college are long forgotten. This one gives me something to talk about.

There is an ancient Chinese folktale that beautifully illustrates this principle. Now, as I encounter what seems to be a misfortune in my life, I return to the central images of this story and am reminded of how inconclusive every event truly is. Here's my version of the tale.

THE REMARKABLE HORSE

Long ago an old, sickly man and his son lived in an impoverished village. Luckily for the old man, his son was healthy and strong, otherwise they would surely have perished. One day while they were working in their barn, a magnificent wild horse unexpectedly rode into their stable. The father motioned to the son to quickly close the gate. For such a poor farmer this was a stroke of incredible luck and good fortune. No one in the village had ever seen such a brilliant animal, and certainly it would fetch a very high price at the market. A neighbor stopped by to visit, remarking to his elderly friend that this was a fortunate happening. Certainly the gods were smiling with favor on him this day. The old man's response surprised him. Stroking his beard, he said, "Perhaps this is good fortune. Perhaps it's not. Only time will tell."

Sure enough, just three days later the horse jumped over the fence and was gone. Once again the neighbor stopped by to commiserate with his friend and commented on what bad luck it was that the horse had escaped. But the old man just stroked his beard and echoed his words of a few days earlier, "Perhaps it is bad fortune, and then again, perhaps it's not. Only time will tell."

A week passed. While the old man and his son were repairing their house, they heard what sounded like a stampede. Sure enough, it was a whole herd of wild horses led by the magnificent horse that had escaped only a few days before. He led them into the corral and the old man's son quickly ran to close the gate. As before, when the neighbor heard of this miraculous event, he stopped by and commented to his friend on his good fortune. The old man just shook his head, muttering, "Perhaps this is good fortune, but perhaps it's not. Only time will tell."

How prophetic his words were. The next day his son was attempting to break in one of the new horses and was thrown.

His leg was shattered in two places. The village doctor was hopeful in his diagnosis, saying that the young man would walk again after he fitted a tight brace around his thigh and shin. But he warned that it would require many months of healing and rest. Given his arthritis and fragile back, this was bad news for the old man. He had grown to depend on his son for help with many of the more difficult chores on the farm. What was he to do now? As you might expect, the neighbor visited to express his regret about the accident and to declare what an unfortunate turn of events this had been. But the old man patiently replied, "Perhaps this is bad fortune, but then again, maybe it's not. Only time will tell."

Two weeks later a regiment of soldiers rode into the village. A war was brewing with a northern province, and they conscripted every young man to fight, except, of course, the old man's son, who was too incapacitated to even be considered. Not one of those men returned alive from the war. The old man's son eventually healed and was once again able to help his father. And, as the wise father often said after his son was spared the fate of so many other young men, "We never know whether a thing is good or bad until the story is finished."

When we take this inconclusive outlook of time, seeing every event as part of a continuous whole, understanding becomes possible. With this perspective, every instant is capable of being redeemed from nothingness and made into something meaningful. This is wisdom. Some find it earlier than others.

Can there be an ultimate meaning? If there is such a thing, I believe it may be discovered only at the very end, as life ebbs from our bodies and time as we know it draws to a close. In these final moments, we are best equipped to draw the last conclusion about what was good and what was bad, what was relevant and what was immaterial. At this time, even our suffering can be proudly owned and understood as a teacher of sorts, a defining condition of life that brought us deep meaning and perspective while wearing the guise of pain.

Looking Forward to Look Back

As we grow older, it seems to be more important to look back than to look forward, to see our life in all its dimensions as a story. This shift in perspective starts for most of us in our forties and fifties. While we plan for retirement and look forward to the emotional and financial relief of having finished rearing children, we are predisposed to reminisce about the very conditions we couldn't wait to escape. This is not just some idle trick of the mind or a sign of an unfulfilled life. Rather, storying our lives plays a crucial role in personal development and should be taken seriously. Constructing and reconstructing narratives that weave a wholeness out of the parts of our lives is a significant and worthwhile endeavor. Interestingly, the word "narrate" is related to the Greek word *gnoscere*, to know. Creating narratives that are filled with our life experiences may be the only way we can know and understand our journey through this world.

We must enter this endeavor with the compassion of a playwright who loves all the characters, seeing every shortcoming and blemish as a necessary component of an interesting storyline. A life with no failures, no deep character flaws, no losses, no scars, and no unresolved issues is not only unrealistic, it's undesirable and, ultimately, boring. The ideal life portrayed in ads for every product imaginable perpetrates a myth of painless living. This is the stuff of fairy tales filled with wishful thinking and "happily ever after" endings.

As with any decent piece of literature, our story must also reveal who we and the other players are through our actions, not through encapsulated descriptions. Neatly illustrated explanations that reduce emotions and conflicts to psychodynamic interpretations not only make for bad history, they create stilted and stuck lives. We are first and foremost our stories. Attempts at rigid categorizations rob us of our dignity and uniqueness.

Today it's not unusual to hear people identify themselves as "co-dependent," "dysfunctional," "an adult child of . . ." These attributes may have their place in helping a person recognize that there is an antecedent to present-day problems, and gilded tales of a wonderful childhood may, in fact, be hiding more faithful renditions of the truth. Ultimately, though, when these explanations are swallowed whole (as many people seem to be doing), they are a disservice to anyone who wishes to truly understand themselves. They are story killers, squashing any opening for genuine exploration and redemption. Unfortunately, they are also deep ruts in the road that grab the least suspecting wagon's wheels, producing a train of followers who lose themselves in a flat story preordained and constructed by others. If you have ever attended a twelve-step meeting, you will find diehards who for years have been telling the same story over and over. While these stories may at first be liberating, with time they can enslave.

With a dispassionate attitude, we must be willing to look at ourselves as revealed through our stories. Is the protagonist someone admirable or loathsome? Likable or despicable? Understandable or an enigma? When we review the many difficulties endured by this person, were these challenges met courageously? How did cowardice serve our protagonist, and what opportunities were missed because he or she lacked the guts to take action? Do we like this individual more for the stands he or she took in life? Can we find forgiveness for the failures of character and the times when pragmatism overruled honored principles? Do we like how he or she dealt with people? Seeing the past in the context of the many events that followed, does it all make sense?

In this way we compose a picture that clarifies who we have been in the world. Out of these stories and judgments we find our identity. It may not fit the ideal most of us would like to hold up to the mirror, but it is ours and ours alone.

Just as cultural myths help a people make sense of the powerful and frequently destructive forces that rule the natural world and human affairs, personal and familial stories take on a comparable mythic quality. Incomprehensible decisions, and even destructive behavior, can all be accepted when couched in a narrative with a beginning, a middle, and an end. The internal motivations of the protagonist and the supporting cast may not always be revealed, but at least the meanings of their actions can be seen and appreciated, however painful the consequences.

In their depth, these stories help us to discover our persona as hero. The outward search for models on the football field, basketball court, and silver screen masks our deep desire to step onto the heroic stage ourselves. By idolizing others, we denigrate our own triumphs. By devoting our lives to emulating another's path, we rob our own souls of a more satisfying fulfillment. At the conclusion of such a life, whose story is it? The tragedy is that many of us become nothing more than bit players in our own play.

We must step onto the stage. Engage the other actors. Innocently act without preset conclusions. And, with time, we must look back over our shoulder, wondering at the meaning of it all, healing ourselves by telling the tale. This is the gift of story.

CHAPTER 4

Healing Words

And so the curse was lifted,
According to the tale;
One kiss, and a prince stood there
Where a toad had been.
It is possible . . . such a strain,
Under the kiss of the harrow,
Could suffice. As when a man
Clutches his ears, deafened
By his world, to find a jewel
Made of pain in his hands.
   —Thomas Kinsella, "Folk Wisdom"

Many years ago, I was trapped in Glacier National Park by a fierce blizzard. Wind roared past our camp throughout the night. By morning, the temperature had dropped, and we were stuck in a fog bank that whirled by us and disappeared behind a white curtain.

We headed out that day walking head-on into a fifty-mile-an-hour gale with snow and hail pocking our ruddy complexions. Four inches of snow and ice accumulated on the windward side of our packs and clothes in less than ten minutes. I realized that we could die out here and that no one would find us until the next June, when the snows melted. Huddling together like cattle taking their last stand against a predator, we debated our options and decided to turn back. It was a good thing. The wind whipped harder, and at times I leaned into it with all my weight just to keep both feet on the trail. We struggled to make our way to the few lonesome trees that had guarded our previous night's stay. After setting up the tents, we stripped off our soaking gloves, pants, hats, and boots and slipped into our down bags to wait for a break in the weather. Except for a brief dinner of English muffins and peanut butter—and the miserable task of hanging our food out of the bears' reach—we stayed in those bags for nearly twenty hours.

All night, snow pelted the tent's outer protective skin, and wind ricocheted off the mountains, racing with the speed of an avalanche toward our precarious nest in the trees. Occasionally, the sound of thunder, or of a huge boulder tumbling over a cliff, echoed throughout the valley.

Sometime around sunrise the snow stopped. I decided to venture out. Our packs were barely visible beneath the drifts that had accumulated around the tent. I walked to the pit toilet and was relieved to find our food still hanging from its perch. Not even the bears were willing to brave such a storm. The metal toilet seat was cold, and my legs quivered as goose bumps crept up my ankles to my thighs. It was good to be out of the tent, even if it meant sitting half naked in the frigid air. On the floor was an old spy novel left behind by a previous occupant. I was too weary to pick it up.

One by one, my friends struggled into the light. With miserable looks in our eyes, and hands and feet hurting from the wet and the cold, we tried desperately to get warm.

Everything was wet. Our spirits were nearly broken. No one wanted to admit it, but this wilderness was just too tough for us.

We hiked out that day. Quietly. Our shoulders were weighed

down by the trials of the last twenty-four hours, and the thirteen treacherous miles that day left my muscles screaming and
my toes aching.

"A Jewel Made of Pain"

I would not wish the above circumstances on anyone, and I
would certainly never want to repeat it again. But the very act
of telling you this story changes the way I see these events, al-
tering the way I feel. What may have been the most miserable
twenty-four hours I have ever spent has been exalted into something worth celebrating. I and my friends survived, living to tell
about our brush with disaster, none the worse for wear, and prepared to tackle the wilderness once more.

By telling you about my trip to Glacier, I have taken the stuff
of suffering and transformed it into one of the most elemental
and important materials of human existence—meaning. By
telling the story, I am no longer the victim of circumstances beyond my control. I have wrested back control by the simple act
of description, turning what seems to be a failure in almost
every way into a heroic saga of survival. In this manner, even
acute suffering can be redeemed.

A few years ago, I heard the story of Arn Chorn, a teenage
refugee from the Cambodian war and the horrific slaughter per-
petrated by the Khmer Rouge. His journey of healing is a mon-
ument to what is possible in each of our lives.

Arn's parents were killed by the Khmer Rouge, who viciously
drove city dwellers into the fields to work. Many of the children
who survived these forced marches were made to act as human
shields for the soldiers. Their life expectancies were, obviously,
short.

While in one of the camps, Arn watched as his sister slowly
died of dysentery. He had also witnessed many of his other relatives die in this way. When he was forced to leave for another

camp, he had no choice but to desert her. Tearfully, Arn departed, his heart rent with sadness, remorse, and guilt. He never saw her again.

It was at this moment when he realized that his fate would be the same if he remained. He fled through the forest to the safety of Thailand. It was the Khmer Rouge's policy to hunt down escapees. If they weren't executed, they would be returned to the camps and watched more vigilantly. The soldiers were not far behind when Arn made it past his last obstacle to freedom—a swiftly flowing river.

While Arn was in a refugee camp, Reverend Peter Pond befriended and eventually adopted him, bringing him to the United States. Even though he now lived in a safe, supportive world filled with material comforts, Arn could find little reason for joy, much less a desire for continuing his life. His despair was overwhelming.

One day while driving with Arn, a mutual friend, Judith Thompson, asked him to describe the circumstances of his flight from the Khmer Rouge. Until this time, he had not shared with anyone the burden of his decision, made years before. Weeping, he described every step of his escape. With a long history in peer counseling, Judith listened intently and with compassion. During the many weeks that followed, Arn shared his story over and over with Judith, each time revealing a new detail that had been covered by the weight of guilt and shame. With each sharing, Arn experienced a sense of freedom that he had not felt since coming to this country—one that flowed from within.

The powerful transformation Judith witnessed in Arn led her to ask two simple questions that transformed both her life and Arn's—what if other children who had been deeply wounded by war were able to share their experiences with each other? And, what would it be like for children from this country to hear these stories and the details of the abominable conditions that are the by-products of the violent conflicts initiated by adults?

Thus was born Children of War, a nonprofit, international effort that brought together children from strife-torn countries around the world. By sharing their stories with each other, and in forums at schools throughout the States, these children were able to make the face of war real for so many of us who are desensitized to violence and conflict. Their pain no longer seemed to be a senseless suffering. It had found meaning and purpose. Now, because of their pain, they could serve the world as witnesses of war. As their despair was "storied," they were able to find a common bond. Alchemically, their stories released them to fully experience the birthright of childhood—joy. We, too, regardless of the nature and depth of our suffering, can rediscover the roots of connection, healing, love, and joy by courageously telling our own tales that are filled with grief, pain, and distress.

Finding a Place of Wholeness

As our world moves and shakes beneath our feet, we are challenged daily to find new ways of coping with and making sense of it all. Needing to ground ourselves in the realities at hand, while also searching for a perspective that allows us to find purpose in the events, feelings, and ideas that surround us, we desperately need tools that can help us keep it all together, giving a sense of wholeness to what would otherwise be a fractured reality.

The narrative structure of story impresses understandable patterns of meaning on experience, no matter how discontinuous an event is with our core beliefs and current view of things. This shows up most vividly in the midst of personal crises.

A friend of mine who works as a chaplain at a local hospital described for me what happens when an unconscious trauma victim is brought into the emergency room. Frequently the patient's identity is unknown, and lifesaving procedures are initiated while a chaplain or social worker attempts to contact the next of kin (if other family members weren't also involved in the accident). But it's not unusual for a parent or sibling to be informed in a more dramatic fashion.

In one case, a mother was driving by the scene of an accident. One of the cars that was mangled looked quite familiar, much like the one belonging to her teenage daughter. As she got closer, she realized that it *was* a family member's car. Frantically she pulled her vehicle to the shoulder, asking every emergency worker within earshot what had happened. The ambulance had pulled away moments before. She implored those who were first on the scene for details. The shock of the realization practically incapacitated her. She furiously questioned anyone who could give her information: "How did it happen? Who was at fault? In what direction was my daughter's car going? How fast was the other driver going? What condition was she in when they put her in the ambulance? Is she alive? What are the chances she's going to be okay? She *is* going to be okay, isn't she?"

Before anyone could answer her questions, she pulled back into traffic, racing to catch up with the ambulance. As she entered the emergency room, they were wheeling her daughter into the operating suite. What did she do?

According to my friend, she began talking with whomever she could find, recounting the horrible details of the event, struggling with how this could happen to her beautiful daughter. And she was not satisfied with telling the tale just once. Over and over she recounted what had happened. She appraised the event from every possible angle.

Each attempt at description represented a quest to digest the horrid consequences of her daughter's accident. Such storytelling can go on for hours, even days. Repeatedly, persons who are traumatized recount the relevant events to anyone with a willing ear. What these people need most at this time is generosity of listening. They don't require sedatives, psychoanalysis, or even reassurance; it's the patience of someone who is willing to say, "Now, tell me again where you were when the drunk driver ran that stop sign," that gives them the space to begin healing the pain.

This scenario plays itself out daily in emergency rooms throughout the world. It is not specific to gender or age. Universally, human beings will resort to narrative to come to grips with a shattered reality.

In less severe circumstances, the principle also holds true. The only thing missing is the urgency, but the need is there just the same. Representing our world to others through story is innately human, as crucial to our soul's survival as breathing is to the survival of our body. Short-circuit this natural process and you will witness all forms of disease. It may show up as a physical symptom or as mental distress. More likely, it will appear under the guise of a nameless anxiety, or a general depression that we can't seem to attribute to anything in particular. These are the symptoms of an un-storied life.

Many things in our lives cry out to be storied—unfinished relationships, momentous changes that affect the course of our existence, and unjust hurts at the hands of friends and parents. In my experience, the events that need most to be storied are the emotional equivalents of car accidents that could never be spoken about or shared because of fear or shame. The wounds of sexual and physical abuse are prime examples of what could be healed with a minimum of scarring if the victims felt the safety to immediately "story" the event, much as relatives of trauma victims do. But humiliation and fear of retribution prevent the child from speaking his or her truth, and the trauma goes underground, now living outside conscious awareness, emerging in all sorts of dysfunctional ways. If the adult is willing to return to the event, recover the memories, translate them into story form, and speak them to a committed listener (in this case, usually a psychotherapist), the event can be redeemed, even transformed alchemically into a jewel made of pain. But it may require years of telling and retelling in conjunction with other healing modalities until the metamorphosis is complete, a new equilibrium is found, and the person once again discovers wholeness within. To weave together the slender threads of a torn life into a firm pattern of meaning can give even the most pernicious emotional and physical injuries a role of honor in our experience. This is the power of story.

CHAPTER 5

The Listening Way

Plunging into the world of hidden memories can be like dredging a dark and foreboding deep well. These things we describe, often dripping with emotion and covered over by algae and years of encrustation, only become clearer as we speak about them. At first, they seem useless, barely worth all this attention. Why would anyone care to listen? Memories seem so banal and ordinary, hardly deserving mention. Little do we know that they contain power and energy that can infuse our lives with beauty and meaning. It's just that they masquerade as meaningless fragments of a broken life. Beneath this facade are the seeds for vitality and wholeness itself.

To unveil this deceptive guise, we need a priestess—someone who can perform one of the most mystical and profound rituals known throughout the ages. While this ceremony can be performed at almost any time, requiring only two individuals, it is best accomplished within the context of a ritual space. To be truly effective, it requires a particular attention to detail that few individuals are capable of giving. This ritual is what we call "listening." But this word does not do justice to the depth and power of the act. Because there is listening, and then there is *listening*.

53

Sacred Speech and Listening
for a Falling Branch

Listening in the first sense is something we do each day. But it's not really listening at all. It's more akin to filtering and screening. Selectively, we exclude from our attention all the things that are not useful to our purpose or the task at hand. This is not listening, but rather *using* the world of experience and the people who inhabit this world to carry out our various agendas.

If you were to bring the delicate world of your memory to a person who listens like this, it's unlikely that you would get more than a few paces down the road of sharing. Reminiscing for such a listener has little to do with his survival in the world, nor does he appreciate the inner world of the teller and the destructive consequences of interrupting someone's sharing. Such a listener's failure can be communicated by as little as a furrowed brow or a habitual glance at a clock.

On the other hand, real listening is the creation of a sacred space in which another's words are contained and transformed into hallowed speech. Like remembering, this form of listening is also intentional. Such a listener recognizes the responsibility involved, understanding that performing the ritual with an attention to the minutest detail can create the conditions for the healing of the speaker.

What is this like? I sit across from a friend having a cup of tea in a small café. We are talking about an earlier time in our lives in which we spent long periods each day in the woods. It's a simple sharing—nothing of seeming importance on the surface. But it was during these quiet times among the trees that we each were happiest as children and most at home in ourselves. My friend can listen to me in one of several ways. She can look for the common threads of our experience, searching to fit my memories into her own broad story. I may suddenly find myself competing for equal time in the conversation. Pieces of my story become co-opted into hers. My words mean nothing to her other than as echoes of her own thoughts. Off she runs with stories of the woods, leaving me at the edge of the forest. I feel empty, lost, and unimportant.

In another scenario, my friend could offer me something different. As I speak of sitting on a large rock by a stream, watching three caterpillars inch their way up the stone, her eyes encourage me to say more. I can see that she is seeing the little creatures as vividly as I do. Her face expresses delight in my every word and feeling. She asks me to tell her more about their black-and-orange backs, and describe in clearer detail their furry bodies, and to tell again how they abruptly stopped in their tracks as the cracking sound of a falling tree branch resounded through the forest. I feel heard, respected, and cared for. This is *listening*. It is so powerful that it can lend importance to a simple sharing and bring dignity to even the smallest detail of my past.

Each of us needs to be heard in this way. It takes so little to be a willing listener, but within our institutions, families, and communities, real listening is often a casualty of change. For the elderly, a failure to be heard can even be fatal. In *How Can I Help?*, Ram Dass and Paul Gorman echo this sentiment through the painful plea of a nursing-home resident.

> Heard. . . . If they only understood how important it is that we be heard! I can take being in a nursing home. It's really all right, with a positive attitude. My daughter has her hands full, three kids and a job. She visits regularly. I understand.
>
> But most people . . . they just want to tell their story. That's what they have to give, don't you see? And it's a precious thing to them. It's their life they want to give. You'd think people would understand what it means to us . . . to give our lives in a story.
>
> So we listen to each other. Most of what goes on here is people listening to each other's stories. People who work here con-

sider that to be . . . filling time. If they only knew. If they'd just take a minute to listen.

Listening is soul work. It can help the living find the meaning to go on in the midst of trying circumstances, and it can help the dying accept the brevity of their lives. Without listening, there can be no story. And without stories, we cannot complete the unfinished work of healing.

The Listener's Secret Gift

The healing touch of storytelling reaches deeply into the listener's heart as well, indelibly imprinting there the mark of the story and its message, weaving the listener into the dance of community. As the listener witnesses the teller, receiving the story, she is not passively absorbing the words that are spoken. Listeners are not empty receptacles, listlessly waiting to be filled according to the output of the speaker. Rather, the process of listening is both active and creative.

When a setting is described, the teller is first seeing it in all its detail, playing the memory like a movie in his mind's eye. Likewise, the listener translates the teller's words back into the language of pictures, sensations, and feelings, reconstructing in her own unique way descriptions of a burning barn, or a raging storm, or a father holding a child close to his heart. No doubt, as you read these words, you also saw the barn, the storm, and the father and child. But was your barn made of old wood like mine, first emitting a warm glow before suddenly bursting into an explosive fire? Your storm a squall line moving quickly across a calm bay that erupted into a boiling cauldron as the cloud front passed overhead? Your father a dark-skinned man cradling a blond-haired boy with tears running down his cheeks?

In all likelihood, you saw each of these differently than I did. That's the beauty of the human mind. We each have a dialect that is all our own, uniquely equipped to render words into a private language of images. But this dialect is not entirely private. It shares a common structure with the dialects of the rest of the people who inhabit our community. This structure allows us to find approximate images that resemble the pictures others carry in their memories. They're not exact, but close enough in form and in meaning to make it possible for us to know and understand what others think, see, and feel.

Through listening to stories, we are joined with the teller in a remarkable dance that opens us up to new places, people, and ideas. More important, stories become the vehicle for transmitting a whole range of experiences from the teller, experiences that can become part of the landscape of the listener's experience.

When you hear my story, it is transformed into a tale that feels intimately like your own, even palpably real and personal, especially if you repeat it to another. This is most apparent in the case of fairy or folk tales, but I believe it is true in the case of personal stories as well. After a few tellings, it no longer matters from where these anecdotes and tales originated. They take on a life of their own, permeating our experiences. The original teller is like an apparition, standing behind us as we speak, becoming less and less important to the tale upon each retelling. The places I have traveled can live and breathe as memories within you. The people who have touched my heart and filled my life with joy can become like friends to you as you hear tales of their adventures and misadventures. My misfortunes can be shared by you, as much a cause for you to cry as for me. Joyful events can uplift you to the same extent that my spirits have been uplifted. All you need do is recall the events that left me doubled over with laughter, and you, too, will be laughing wholeheartedly.

Such is the stuff of empathy—the glue that holds families and cultures together. Without having to experience the dire consequences of another's actions, we enter into the lessons and meaning a particular experience embodied by simply hearing the story. In this way, another's healing journey can create a space of healing within us.

If we are feeling bereft of community, suffering from the isolation that contemporary life breeds, part of what we are truly missing are communal stories that link us to others in the world. Also missing is a sharing circle that gives us a forum for speaking and hearing these tales. Children today are most susceptible to the dangers that occur when our culture creates such a vacuum. I have always felt that the absence of heroic tales to guide young persons through the rocky waters of adolescence is a major contributor to teen suicide. The heroic myths are filled with vivid accounts of male and female initiation, confrontations with injustice, grappling with one's fate, as well as how to slay dragons and withstand the torments of sirens who beckon from rocky shores. Through metaphorical language, these stories can frame for the listener the psychic and spiritual dilemmas plaguing his or her mind and soul. They also offer hope and powerful images of perseverance, cunning, bravery, and triumph. Where are teens to turn today for such guidance in the face of despair? Parents do not know the ancient tales. How many are in touch with their own hero's journey? They have no well to draw from, no source for healing wisdom. What can they offer other than empty words of encouragement that do little to nourish a young soul? This is why every great teacher since the beginning of time has drawn on the world of parables to guide journeyers who have no map, compass, or sextant. Ironically, these parables can heal young listeners with the medicinal herb of metaphor, leading them simultaneously inward and onward. To affirm our inner reality and our place of belonging in the outer world, we must hear stories.

The Deserving Tale

Recently I returned from Wales, where I led a program on how to discover and create personal and family narratives. In Britain, there has been little emphasis on this genre of story. For reasons that have to do with the character of the people and their comfort level when sharing personal material with strangers, the British seem to feel much more at home in the territory we call traditional tales. For better or worse, I was there to share with them the gospel of how every event in our lives is material that can be woven into a story worth telling.

During the workshop, I wasn't certain how well this approach was being received. The English are not particularly demonstrative. There were a few signs, though, that I had gotten through. After participants had mapped out the neighborhoods of their childhood, one woman in her fifties privately shared with me a forgotten memory of her last days with her parents, both diplomats, before they departed for Africa. It was the custom at that time to not bring children on these assignments. Instead, they were enrolled in boarding schools. At the age of seven, she enjoyed Christmas with her mom, who left the next day. For the remainder of the holiday she stayed with family friends before being shipped off to a very uncertain and frightening future.

Her most vivid memory of this time was of the father of this family testing the rope ladder that would be used in case of a fire. As it dangled from the third-story window, she fantasized about escaping in the middle of the night, quietly climbing down it while everyone else slept. In a vague plan, she remembers dreaming of a long adventure culminating in a reunion with her mother and father in Africa.

When she concluded this story, she shyly asked me, "Is this story worth telling?" There were such strong images here, and I could see that she had opened a window to a pivotal time in her life that was begging for healing. This was not only a story worth telling, it was a tale that needed to be heard. With her permission I shared it with the group. Its universal appeal brought tears to others' eyes. They, too, had experienced the same deep wound. The story, though unfinished, spoke eloquently to a place in each listener that pleaded for exploration and healing.

As the week progressed, this perspective was vindicated by Hugh Lupton, a respected English storyteller. He shared with the group how story is seen in many West African villages. At dusk, the people gather around a central fire. Conversation is casual, moving from the events of the day to tales of personal recollection. As the darkness closes in on the villagers, an elder fondly remarks on how he remembers a young man's grandfather, sharing a marvelous tale that touched him. Stories of those who have passed on begin to fill the night air. As the stars appear in the sky, these stories are replaced by tales of the ancestors. Legendary exploits are reverently recounted. Onward through the night the stories are woven together, legends giving way to folktales, then to wonder tales filled with magic and mystery. By early morning, the ancient myths are retold for those who are still awake. Finally, as dawn approaches, stories of the Creator's miraculous work are repeated. Even though everyone has heard these stories many times before, they are still relished. Through story, each member of the community is personally linked back in time to the very beginning of the universe.

This progression of story is known as the "Ladder to the Moon." Every rung is significant, providing a foundation for the tales that follow. How interesting it is that the first step deals with the world of stories drawn from personal experience.

As the week in Wales progressed, I believe this insight led to others privately seeking me out. Each conversation started out with an apology for intruding, quickly seguing into a query to see if I might have a moment to judge as to whether an anecdote was worth sharing with another.

On the last night, during a performance intermission, one of the participants asked if she could have a word with me. As we sat outside, she spoke in fits and starts while holding back her tears.

What unfolded was an amazing tale that spanned three continents. At the age of fourteen, while living in a small village in Denmark, she had read of the plight of the Vietnamese children who had escaped in the last hours before the fall of Saigon. Many had ended up in Camp Pendleton in California before being relocated throughout the States. She was moved by their challenges and suffering and decided to address a letter to all of them. The response was both unexpected and overwhelming. Hundreds of letters began arriving at her doorstep. One in particular caught her attention. It was written by a young man her same age, and she was deeply touched by his story.

With time, they continued their correspondence, and she grew to love him as a brother. Finally, at the age of nineteen, she traveled to the States and was able to meet him.

In the last ten years she's lost touch with her pen pal and no longer knows where he lives. Desperately, she'd like to find him and reestablish communication. But she's afraid even to try. What if he has changed? If he is married, will his wife understand the sisterly love she feels for him?

As the lights flashed for the resumption of the performance, she wanted to know if she should write this story. Would anyone else care about the silly tale of a young girl who fell in love with a young boy from halfway around the world?

My answer was simple. In fact, it's the same answer I give to everyone who is willing to make this inward journey: It is a deserving tale.

Even if she never finds him again, by telling the story to me, and hopefully to others, she will discover a piece of herself that was lost in the mail, address unknown, undelivered. In the night air, she began climbing the ladder to the moon, discovering that her story is her destination.

PART TWO

On the Path

CHAPTER 6

First Steps

I have a good friend, Ron Fell, who is better prepared than anyone I know when it comes to backpacking trips. About four weeks before the appointed date, I receive a detailed checklist of all the items I'll need while in the wilderness. Some of these are necessities like three pairs of underwear, two pairs of woolen socks, a parka, a set of utensils, a knife, a compass, and most important, a topo map that clearly shows the trails and preferred camping sites. Other pieces of equipment are for those "just in case" dangers that the wilderness often dishes up—a blanket made of space-age materials to quickly warm up a body suffering from hypothermia, a trash bag to cover the pack in the event of rain, a snakebite kit, and loud bells to scare off grizzly bears. Not to bring these items would be foolhardy, if not even dangerous.

Venturing into the territory of memory and the past requires nearly as much preparation. You need the right equipment for survival, and special tools for traversing difficult terrain. Because many of the social mechanisms that support storytelling in other cultures are absent in our own, part of your journey must include the creation of special rituals within your own family and community to support your efforts. If your interpersonal network does not champion the practice of storytelling, it's unlikely that you will ever harvest the deep fulfillment when "story" is a regular part of your daily life and sharing. This chapter lays the groundwork for this task.

Creating a Storytelling Tradition

For many of us, storytelling was not a regular part of our childhood experience. We didn't grow up with uncles weaving tales on our front porches (most of us didn't even have front porches) or neighbors gathering around the hearth to tell stories, sing songs, dance, or recite poetry. To participate with family and friends in this way can be the most natural and fulfilling thing in the world. But for those of us who are uninitiated into the world of story, it can be incredibly awkward if we take the responsibility for creating the experience for others.

In Ireland and Scotland there is a wonderful model for how to begin this tradition in your home. They call it a *Ceilidh* (pronounced "kaley"). In most older villages, at least one home was known as the *Ceilidh* house. On regular intervals, usually weekly, the whole community was invited to gather there to share stories and songs. The host was responsible for setting the tone of the evening by telling the first tale, dancing the first jig, or reciting an original poem or verse from one of the traditional masters.

By bringing story into the regular fabric of everyday life, your children are taught intimately and subtly how all experience is essentially a storied affair. Perhaps for the first time in their adult lives, grown-ups are also given permission to enter the world of personal memory and imagination. Both child and adult will find their imaginations ignited by the tales that are shared. Miraculously, you, your family, and friends will be woven into a web of unanticipated closeness that will enhance any notion you had of what community is all about.

A few years ago, I launched many such events in my own home. Purposefully, I didn't invite any professional storytellers. With a playful invitation, I urged my friends and acquaintances to bring any story of their choosing—from their own personal experience, one they had heard and liked, or a literary tale from a book. Many people would call me a few days before the event to RSVP and inquire if it was all right if they didn't share. That was fine. I encouraged them, though, to come and bring their generous listening. Invariably, once they had warmed to the safe and relaxing setting, one after another would venture forward, having been reminded of a long-forgotten event in his or her own life.

Every evening would develop a theme of its own, spurred on by story after story that arose from something someone else had shared. Once it was outrageous experiences in Turkish baths. Another night we gravitated toward stories of au pairs. Sometimes people would bring a favorite children's story or myth to read. We even had some people share poetry.

Most of those who attended would never identify themselves as storytellers. Nor did they leave those evenings with any belief that they were prepared to perform professionally on stage. But when they did depart, which was usually very late, they were sated, as if they had participated in an eight-course meal. This was not your ordinary cocktail party. Many people would linger, hoping that someone else would uncork another exciting story. The evenings were intoxicating. For weeks afterward, friends would comment about the experience. Those who couldn't make it expressed deep regrets, having heard secondhand of the rich stories that had been served up.

There are many naturally occurring opportunities for a *Ceilidh*. Family reunions, which usually devolve into large feasts with the men watching sports while the women prepare food in the kitchen, can take on a very different complexion when storytelling is given a primary role. A friend of mine recently gathered his extended family for two days. With my encouragement, he decided to introduce storytelling into the evening's events. His mother was there, and, like many families today, his and his wife's children from previous marriages were there along with their children. They decided to all share their earliest memories of their favorite foods. Even the young ones got their turn.

As Dave contemplated his past, he settled on a memory of his mother baking apple pie. It was her custom to take the trimmed dough from the crust and sprinkle sugar and cinnamon on it, then stick it in the oven to bake. These treats were a reward for his patience. As he shared this memory, not only did it nourish his soul in a very real way, but he looked across the room at his mother, who had tears in her eyes. It was a special moment for her as well.

People enjoyed themselves so much that they insisted on picking another theme for sharing the following evening. More and more families that I know are following this model. They are surprised by the simple joy inherent in the act of sharing their stories.

The First Rung of the Ladder

Earlier I mentioned the West African tradition of climbing the "Ladder to the Moon." This also provides a wonderful example for building a storytelling tradition. Start your evening by sharing the events of the day—the new and good along with the painful and frustrating experiences. There's great wisdom in "storying" the everyday happenings in our lives. Unfinished conversations at work are given an avenue for airing and exploration. The nagging details of matters that require further attention have a chance to be brought into the light of awareness instead of subliminally festering in our dreams. These stories are the foundation for the more involved tales that follow.

Moving from the present into the near past creates a window on a time and place that takes on mythic importance in our lives.

As we share these stories of long ago, and others' memories are spurred on in the same direction, those gathered together begin to build a bond of closeness made of common pains, losses, and joys. Our individual pasts no longer seem so solitary. We discover that others have been down similar roads, dealt with the same challenges, and succumbed to identical temptations.

Those who have passed on can then take center stage. Their place in our lives is revealed through our stories of their accomplishments and failures. By celebrating the "dearly departed" through story, we bring them into our circle of familiarity, almost as though they fill the empty seats in the room. In this way, our sense of community is expanded longitudinally across time. When the ancestors are with us, we need never feel lonely.

From the ancient ones, we move into the murky world of legends. These can be both familial and cultural. If you have a penchant for genealogy, you can trace your past all the way back to a fanciful figure who may seem bigger than life. If not, explore the many legends that people your cultural or national past. In these stories, you can find small traces of yourself along with your many aspirations and hopes. You can also discover the meaning of courage and other important virtues. In the process, your community circle will once again be expanded and enriched.

Today, most folk literature has been transcribed from the oral medium into writing. Ironically, for most of us this attempt at preservation has taken it out of the realm of living and breathing reality. The task for our culture is to reencode these stories into the oral language, helping them to again breathe and live. This rung of the ladder takes us beyond the personal into an exploration that must, at the same time, be personally relevant. I suggest that you begin introducing folktales into your sharing circle by finding stories that speak intimately to you. While these stories are about common people who lived in another day and time, they often contain universal concerns and dilemmas that are very relevant to contemporary life. Such stories can powerfully frame issues that would otherwise remain obscured and inaccessible.

Another result of destorification is the loss of magic in our lives. Scientific models of reality and economic necessities have robbed us of the ability to daydream and burrow into our imaginations. But wonder and fairy tales can still transport us on fantastic flights of fantasy, fulfilling one of our most important psychic needs. Bring these delightful tales into your storytelling sessions. Ask participants to close their eyes and let the story take them wherever it wishes. They'll discover that the world of magic is still among us. All we must do is learn to see once again with magic eyes.

Reviving the Mythic Tradition

On the next rung of the ladder we find myths. Today, myths are often viewed as fanciful stories of gods and spirits that are no longer relevant to modern concerns. More often than not, these stories are associated with viewpoints that cannot withstand the glaring light of objective and scientific truth. In our rush for a more impersonal account of our world, we have missed something.

Before contemporary times, natural phenomena were explained in terms every person could fathom. Rocks rolled down mountains because the gods were engaged in battle. Storms brewed on the high seas, swallowing entire ships, because Neptune was displeased with some human transgression. Volcanoes angrily erupted to display the wrath of the deities. Every natural event became relevant to human society, noted for its meaning as a sign or portent of things to come. In this way, people were able to discover their places in the world.

These stories have been replaced by laws and theorems that also explain the "why" of things, but in terms that divorce the natural world from our personal experience. When the volcano literally blows its top, why should I care? The neat equation that explains the physics of this natural disaster does not include the world of human affairs. Do we have a reason for moral and ethical behavior if there are no repercussions or consequences in the bigger world? Even if all the gods have been subsumed under the umbrella of the one God, how else can God speak to us if he/she has been stripped of the power to rough us up a little through natural disasters? In this world, God is relatively impotent, and we are strangers in our own home.

What would it be like if we lived as though the scientific viewpoint is just one explanation? What would happen if we began treating the animals, the rocks, and the trees as family members, believing that their "voices" must also be heard? In 1854, Chief Sealth delivered a speech to his people. Dr. Henry Smith was present and made notes that have since been adapted by film scriptwriter Ted Perry and reproduced in *Thinking Like a Mountain* by John Seed, Joanna Macy, Pat Fleming, and Arne Naess. Listen to the words of Chief Sealth as he addresses the president of the United States. He paints a picture of a world that is real and animated, where we are just one of the slender threads in the fabric.

> The perfumed flowers are our sisters; the deer, the horse, the great eagle, these are our brothers. The rocky crests, the juices of the meadows, the body heat of the pony, and man—all belong to the same family. . . . Whatever befalls the earth befalls the sons of the earth. Man does not weave the web of life, he is merely a strand in it. Whatever he does to the web, he does to himself.

Natural myths can return us to our rightful place in the world. Through these stories we can discover new relations, widening our link to the natural landscape. I encourage you to embrace these stories and play with them. Recast them into contemporary language. Update the characters. Discover the wisdom of ancient eyes and how it can renew our own vision.

In the Beginning . . .

How ironic it is that the highest rung on the "Ladder to the Moon" deals with beginnings. Creation stories are perhaps the oldest genre of tales in any culture, yet their relevance is more contemporary than you might imagine. One of the most cherished stories of any child is that of his or her birth. In this story, a young girl discovers whether or not she was welcomed into the family, and who cared about her arrival. She finds her place in the family's history. Knowing that she was welcomed and that everyone accommodated her arrival, she becomes secure in knowing that she is loved.

So it is with creation stories. They aren't just interesting fantasies about the beginning of time and space. They help us to see that we are welcome members of the family of life; that we have a place and purpose in the world; that the Creator loves us. Such stories play an important role in the life of a people. They are also a fitting conclusion to an evening that began in the present and wove its way back in time.

Whether you climb the "Ladder to the Moon" or host a *Ceilidh,* you are creating a structure in your life that can shape your sharing, giving it a sense of direction and wholeness. These frameworks and rituals can also confer on contemporary family life something that is sorely missing—tradition. Whichever rituals you adopt, you can be assured that there will be many unexpected and profound rewards.

Taking the Time

If you and your family are not accustomed to sharing and telling each other stories, the prospect of making the time for storytelling can be awkward, if not intimidating. Where do you start? What will you say? Who will go first? What do you do if there are uncomfortable silences?

In the beginning you may feel that you don't have a story to tell, or that your life experiences would be of no interest to anyone else. You might wonder why anyone would care to listen to the incidental events that fill the span of your lifetime.

Telling stories is not about historical chronologies. In fact, biographical information such as the dates of births and deaths, weddings and divorces, schools attended, jobs held and lost, illnesses and cures, et cetera, at best provides a backdrop to the meaningful and powerful stories of our lives, which are drawn from commonplace occurrences. Moving and gripping stories often live in the spaces where nothing that seems to be significant is happening. But, by changing the focal depth of our lens, many interesting and valuable details emerge into awareness.

Chronicling our lives with only the conspicuous features of our past is much like crossing boulder fields in the mountains without ever noticing what's beneath them. If you have never done this, imagine giant rocks, many of which are more than ten feet in diameter, piled up by the forces of nature with the same whimsy as a child playing with pebbles. Traversing these boulders is very demanding. Leaping from rock to rock requires all of your free attention. But, if you pause for a moment, listen, and take the time to peek beneath these massive stones, there's a rich and enticing world waiting to be discovered. Marmots, lumbering creatures that look like large hamsters, make their homes in the cracks, along with many other interesting and curious animals. Multicolored lichen, moss, and fragile plants are sprouting everywhere. A host of tiny, iridescent bugs busily scamper about. And, if you're especially quiet, sometimes you can hear a small, hidden stream gurgling as it winds its way toward a mountain lake.

If we take the time to stop, look, and listen, the rich texture of the commonplace events and experiences from the past can

emerge. This is the place to begin. This is where our lives per-
colate and simmer, where the fertile material of the past becomes compost for stories in the present. But if we do not commit ourselves to making the space and time for story, our stories
will remain concealed, and our personal lives will be like those
boulder fields as seen from a distance, filled with a sameness that
is gray and cold.

Making a Place for Story

While it's important to create special times for storytelling
through *Ceilidhs* and family reunions, you can make a space for
story almost anywhere, anytime. For example, I have learned
more from my father while dining out than by sitting quietly in
his living room. One evening in a busy Spanish restaurant he
shared stories for nearly an hour, detailing his experiences during the war, his many attempts at becoming certified to fly in
the army air corps, and how, in order to marry my mother, he
went AWOL for nearly three days without being caught. By offering him my most generous listening, we were able to create
a sacred place in the midst of a mundane setting.

I have found that story can find a home in the most unlikely
situations—long car rides, early morning walks with my wife,
on airplanes sitting next to a complete stranger, and on the
phone with a friend who calls to let me know that something
difficult or tragic has just occurred in his life. Wherever you are
is a place for story.

Setting the Mood

Traditionally, storytelling has occurred naturally when people
congregate. As the numbers increase, often something border-
ing on the mystical can happen, catalyzing the sharing process.

I have sat in the midst of a thousand people at the National Storytelling Festival and felt a spiritual presence that exceeds anything I have ever experienced in a church or synagogue. The simplicity of someone sharing her story seems to invite the sacred into the space.

If there is a magical ingredient that facilitates the flow of stories, it most certainly rests in the mood of the setting. Sitting in tents with hundreds of people at the National Storytelling Festival works because the historic town of Jonesborough, Tennessee, exudes a feeling of nostalgia and friendliness reminiscent of old-time southern hospitality. It's downright folksy, and the closest thing I know to sitting in a cane rocker on someone's front porch while listening to stories of days gone by.

Not all of us have front porches, nor do we all live in locales that can evoke sentimental feelings. But we can create the mood with very little effort. Start by finding a place that is easy and cozy for you, where everyone can relax. It may be around the kitchen table or on the living-room floor with stuffed pillows and beanbag chairs. King-sized beds also make for warm gatherings. Whenever there are more than three or four people present, be sure to sit in a circle. The geometry of sharing is important and ensures that young and old alike can be seen and heard.

Since the beginning of human history, the hearth or central fire formed the center of community life. Food preparation, staying warm, singing, dancing, praying, celebrating, and, of course, storytelling all took place around these fires. The light and heat of burning embers and tales of the ancestors, adventure, and triumphs go hand in hand, creating a powerful mood for sharing. Since the beginning of time, fire and magic have been inextricably linked.

You may not have a fire pit in your backyard or a hearth in your family room, but with a candle you can still bring the warmth of fire into the center of your circle. Turn the lights down low and watch how the dancing flame creates an edge of anticipation as well as an air of relaxation.

One last word of warning—turn off the TV. Our culture is addicted to television, and this may be the single most important factor in the decline of storytelling and family sharing over the last fifty years. Certainly, when we are sick or lonely, TV can be a companion of sorts and can help us forget our misery. But if you've ever walked into a room filled with people watching TV and tried to carry on a conversation, you know it's nearly impossible. Make an agreement to keep the TV off during family sharing times. I promise you, the richness of personal stories will make almost everything on TV pale by comparison.

Ritual Beginnings

There are many significant rituals that can help create a space in which story can thrive. In most oral traditions, there are ceremonial cues tellers use to let listeners know that they are about to enter into a storied space. When we hear the words "Once upon a time," they prepare us to suspend disbelief. In the fantasy that's about to unfold, what's up may be down, people can fly on wings of gold, and fish can walk about dressed in top hats and tails. But we don't object to this topsy-turvy world. Gladly, we give our hand to the teller and are willingly swept away by her words.

My favorite poem for marking the ritual boundaries of worldly and storied reality comes from the Celtic tradition. It goes like this:

> *Under the earth I go.*
> *On the oak leaf I stand.*
> *I ride on the filly that was never foaled.*
> *And, I carry the dead in my hand.*

How do these words speak to you? Where do they take your imagination? For me, these four lines embody every aspect of the healing journey into storytelling. As I move under the earth, I tap into hidden places that have been unconsciously forgotten and delve into parts of myself that are dead and buried. Standing on the uppermost leaf of the oak tree, my vision widens, taking in places and people I might never have known. The filly gives my imagination free rein to travel beyond my comfortable borders. My hands hold ancestors who lived and toiled so that I might become part of their never-ending story.

Norma Livo and Sandra Rietz's *Storytelling: Process & Practice* lists many ritual beginnings and endings used by storytellers from around the world. You'll find it in the recommended reading section. I encourage you playfully to experiment with these beginnings and endings, as well as create new rituals that grow from your family's traditions and history.

Listening—The Heart of Story

There is a real art to listening to a story. In a culture that is preoccupied with the bottom line, we listen to everyday speech by distilling essential information and discarding the rest. Time is of the essence. There is no place for story here.

But communication that is storied demands that we listen as though we have never heard the story before, even if we have. This requires a level of discipline and commitment we're unaccustomed to. If you open yourself to listening in this way, the spirit of the story has a chance to work its way into your soul, speaking to your heart, not just your mind. For receptive listeners, a good story will only get better in the telling.

As simple as it may sound, a story is not a story without at least one outstanding listener. In traditional pueblo life in New Mexico and Arizona, listening is the first and most important step for maintaining their ancient storytelling tradition. If children do not know how to listen, the tribe's stories will never be learned, and the important lessons embodied in these stories will die. Listening is a cultural imperative for Native Americans.

There are many ways to develop and hone your listening powers. While participating a few years ago in *Hama-Ha,* a celebration of Native American storytelling in Santa Fe, I was directed to spend an entire day roaming the desert, just listening. It's remarkable what can happen when you make it your business to focus on only the sounds around you. The whistling and rustling wind became almost deafening. It spoke in a language filled with a rich variety of tones and pitches. Until that day, I never realized how loud my footsteps reverberated on the crusty soil. My ear learned to recognize the sound of small lizards as they scampered in front of my approaching shadow. This is the kind of listening that story requires.

You needn't wander the desert to develop this skill. If your bedroom window opens, sit by it in the morning hours just before sunrise. Birds are already preparing for the day, singing and cooing. Even the sound of traffic possesses its own music. Listen. How many different sounds do you hear? Later in the day, share what you heard with a friend or your spouse.

Experiment when in conversation with another person by purposefully putting aside all of your agendas, rebuttals, and free associations. At first, try it for a couple of minutes. Notice the shape of the person's voice, its pitch, the places that have an edge. Pay attention to the round, soft intonations. Listen with an understanding and compassionate ear. Don't judge. Just hear what the person has to say. Thoughtfully consider its meaning for him. When you attend to another's speech in this way, you may come to recognize the miracle of words. This is sacred listening. To such an ear, story, in all of its forms, is transformed into a melodious language. When the listener is this receptive, both he and the teller are elevated to a new realm of communication. This is the foundation for building trust and safety in any relationship.

There are also practical ways in which to enhance the listening of participants at your *Ceilidhs* or family reunions. Many Native American storytellers employ responsive devices to ensure that their audience's attention is focused on the story at hand. For example, during the story the teller periodically will shout out "Ho," and the audience is expected to respond "Heh." In this way they let the teller know they are listening. When children are present in your sharing circle, this can be a powerful device to keep them involved, present, and participating.

Historically, Native American communities faced many of the organizational problems that contemporary groups experience. Resources were precious and the tribe's survival was dependent on cooperation among all of its members. Whenever an important matter required consideration, the tribe would gather around a central fire to speak what was in their hearts and to listen to the words and wisdom of others. Interestingly, even children had a place in the circle. Their voices were as respected as those of the elders. The tribe's leadership knew that there were some things only young eyes could see.

In these communal discussions, every perspective was valued and decision making was based on a consensual model. If a problem could not be resolved in a manner that was satisfactory to *all* of the members, the matter was tabled for a later time.

In the course of their history, most tribes evolved what we would call parliamentary rules for running these gatherings. Listening was valued above all else. Without generous listening to the ideas and feelings of others, there could be no learning, no vision, no communal future. Perhaps this is where the old saying arose, "Until you walk in the moccasins of another. . . ." Only when we see things through another's eyes can there be understanding and compassion.

To ensure that all were listening, and to guarantee respect for the person speaking, some tribes used devices to command the attention of all who were gathered around the fire. The "talking stick" was one such device. While the speaker was in possession of the stick, she had the floor. All listened until she relinquished the stick to the next person. In this way the talking stick became an important symbol for respecting the views of everyone who discussed matters of import and made decisions that affected the lives of all community members.

Over the last year, I have commissioned a fine artist to create talking sticks for my training programs. She hand-paints dried grapevines in beautiful colors, with abstract designs and symbols. But you don't have to be an artist to craft your own. All you need is a stick, some acrylic paint, and a little imagination.

When you introduce the talking stick into your story circle, share its illustrious history with the group. I have found that people of all ages respond to the stick's meaning and purpose, and that a profound level of respectful listening accompanies its use.

Preserving Your Family Legacy

In my workshops, people always ask whether they should write down family stories or record them on audio or videotape. This is a simple question, but requires an answer that is more than a yes or a no. I want to suggest that none of the above methods for preserving stories is suitable, and call upon the ancient scribe Plato to justify my perspective.

In Plato's *Phaedrus* Socrates tells a story of a time in ancient Egypt when there lived a resourceful god named Theuth. His inventions included calculus, geometry, astronomy, and writing. Thamus, the king, had to approve all innovations before they were introduced to the people. When it came to writing, Theuth was certain he had created something that would improve the wisdom and memory of everyone. Thamus begged to differ.

> "Theuth, my paragon of inventors," replied the king, "the discoverer of an art is not the best judge of the good or harm which will accrue to those who practice it. So it is in this case; you, who are the father of writing, have out of fondness for your off-

spring attributed to it quite the opposite of its real function. Those who acquire it will cease to exercise their memory and become forgetful; they will rely on writing to bring things to their remembrance instead of their own internal resources. What you have discovered is a receipt for recollection, not for memory. And as for wisdom, your pupils will have the reputation for it without the reality: they will receive a quantity of information without proper instruction, and in consequence be thought very knowledgeable when they are for the most part quite ignorant."

Traditional cultures almost always have orally preserved the wisdom of the past. In every generation, at least one person was designated a "keeper of the tales." It was his or her job to learn all the stories going back, at times, for thousands of years. People in these societies were adept at committing to memory voluminous amounts of information that was crucial to surviving in their world. The ancestors weren't historical relics or curios neatly stored away in massive tomes on some shelf. Their stories lived and breathed in the memories of the people.

With regard to storytelling and family heritage, our culture is, at best, orally impaired. Because of our growing reliance on writing everything down or recording it on magnetic tape, we have allowed our oral capacities to slowly atrophy. Wisdom resonates less and less in our personal experience and memory, residing more often in archives and libraries, forgotten and collecting dust.

If you want to truly preserve your family's heritage, you must commit to memory all the stories that you know. This may seem to be a daunting task, but it's easier than you might imagine. The simple act of repeating a story to another person will anchor it in your memory. Telling it two, three, or more times will make it more than just a story about someone else. It will become part of *your* never-ending story. The next step is to find a younger person in your family who is equally as patient and willing to take the time to listen and learn. This is how you can create an enduring family legacy.

For those of you who don't feel you're up to the task, and prefer to rely on more permanent media such as paper, audiotape, or video, I do have a few words of wisdom. First, there are advantages to each. If you or someone in your family likes to write, preserving your life experiences in book form can be a good idea. All too often, though, I hear from elders and their children that they want to write their life stories, but just never quite get around to it. That's because writing is essentially a lonely task, and many of us become obsessed with saying it perfectly. This can chill the creative juices of people who are otherwise quite eloquent.

But there's a deeper process here that short-circuits recollection and reflection. When you sit down to write, there is no listener. In my experience, most people find it a lot easier to talk than write. For this reason, of all the contemporary options for preserving our personal stories, I prefer audio and videotape. Of the two, I favor audiotape because I like a person's stories to live on in my memory, not how he or she looked after a long and exhausting illness, for example.

But I urge you to remember the words of Thamus. I, too, have made the mistake of taping my father's stories, only to allow them to languish on a shelf. Unless you make a commitment to bringing these tapes out on important occasions, like the anniversary of a relative's death or at family reunions, they will become like shadows, lost to future generations.

How to Recapture a Memory and Share It

Earlier I spoke of how we store our past experiences in memory with images or pictures of the things that happened, not with words. These pictures, in all their complexity, become the important keys to our past. Compressed into a simple scene are the secret codes for unlocking memories of conversations, feelings, and even the senses of touch, smell, taste, and hearing. When my friend Dave recalled the episode in his childhood kitchen of his mother baking pies, it drew him into the past by filling him with the aroma of the fruit and the taste of crispy dough covered with cinnamon and sugar. The warm, nostalgic feelings he had for his mother were also present. Emotions, smells, and tastes were instantaneously re-created at a visceral level in the moment when he shared his memory of that scene. I imagine that everyone listening to the story could practically smell the pies baking and taste the cinnamon crisps.

The Mind as Camera

Why we are drawn to particular memories is hard to say. On the surface, it seems to be happenstance. Dave could have as easily remembered a family barbecue or an inedible school lunch. My sense is that our free-association powers cast about like fishing nets with a mesh that allows certain memories to go undetected and others to be captured and brought to the surface of our consciousness. Matters that are currently relevant subliminally affect this search. The fact that Dave was quickly drawn to a past event that included his mother was probably influenced by her presence in the sharing circle, making this recollection doubly meaningful. It's almost as if meaning resides on the membrane of a stored memory, helping the subconscious process of recollection identify whether or not this memory is appropriate to the present moment. In a millisecond it's either deemed worthy or is discarded. But its relevance may only become apparent after it's shared. Even then we are often uncertain as to why something someone is wearing, for example, reminded us of sitting on our grandfather's lap fifty years ago. It's a puzzle that may not be ours to figure out, but simply to witness and appreciate.

Putting psychological and neurological theories aside, at the experiential level recalling something from the past borders on magic. In a famous African tale about Anansi the spider, Anansi returns from the heavens with a magic box filled with stories. This box was the property of Nyami, the sky god, but Anansi earned the right to carry the box back to earth by performing four miraculous tasks. He had to bring to Nyami Onini the boa constrictor, Osebo the giant leopard, Mboro the killer wasp, and Mmotia the fairy no one could see. When Anansi returned, he gathered all his friends in the village to witness the opening of the box and to share its special treats. As he slowly lifted the lid, he thought he saw things squirming around inside. Before he knew it, they had escaped and were flying about the room.

These were all the stories the world would ever know, and as legend has it, Anansi, his wife, Aso, and the villagers were able to grab a few, but most of those stories got away. And people like you and I are still reaching up and pulling stories out of the thin air and telling them to our friends.

Where do stories come from? My experience is like that of the animal people in the tale of Anansi. They're all around us. They're also within us. Sometimes we must labor to earn the right to own them, as did Anansi. Our challenges and achievements become the themes of our stories and our lives. But often all we need do is reach up into thin air and a memory falls into our waiting palm. In the sections that follow, I will show you how to begin the process of harvesting memories from the rarefied atmosphere around and within us, and how simple themes can produce powerful stories.

The Four Elements

In ancient times, fire, water, air, and earth were believed to be the building blocks for all of creation. When people were intimately connected to the forces of nature, their lives were interwoven with the earth as a source of food and protection. But even Mother Earth could be provoked, trembling with anger in the form of an earthquake or a volcano. Water sustained life but could threaten an entire community through raging floods. Wind could fill a fisherman's sails, as well as whip up violent seas. And fire could warm cold hands and cook food, as well as destroy in a minute what took a lifetime to build.

It's not surprising, then, that these elements take on a mythic significance in stories from around the world. They often provide the violent circumstances that test the mettle of a character. And, through their life-sustaining qualities, they supply the stage for a hero's redemption.

Within us, these elements can awaken potent memories, revealing forgotten, yet important, times in our lives. Even if we have constructed an artificial world of bricks, steel, and glass to live in, the suppressed energies of one of these elements in the form of a hurricane or an earthquake will invariably break through to remind us that we cannot live apart from the natural landscape.

But these elements are not just around us. They are within us. After death, our bodies return to the earth, indistinguishable from the dust on the road. And we speak of people who are spacey as "not grounded." The blood that flows through our veins has the same salinity as the oceans, and we characterize days that went well with phrases like "Everything just flowed." The chemical reactions that accompany the digestion of food are similar to the combustion of a fire, and we know that when we are motivated we literally have a "fire in the belly." And we would be as lifeless without breath as the world would be without the wind. Oriental cultures have known for thousands of years that the best barometer for our well-being may be the breath.

Our starting point for recapturing a memory begins with these four elements. In the following sections, I will show you how you can use these simple ideas as guides back to significant moments in your past. You may find that one of these fantasies speaks more powerfully to you than the others. One or more may not speak to you at all. Either way, you are not alone. These differences also show up in the many people whom I've led through these exercises. If, by chance, none of the exercises in the next few pages spurs memories of the past, move on to others in the book. These are, after all, offered as tools and not as tests of your character or power of recollection.

The key to all of these guided fantasies and exercises is to understand that the scenes from the past dance across your awareness, much like a movie projected on the screen of your mind. Telling a story about these events is as easy as seeing the details of these images and describing them before they trail off into the darkness. This is the heart of storytelling, and doesn't require any special skills or innate talents. It's that simple.

You may, of course, at times find it difficult to translate the visual language of pictures into words. Adjectives, nouns, and verbs are often inadequate to do justice to an actual memory. I suggest that you don't overly concern yourself with perfecting the descriptive language of your story. As much as 90 percent of what is communicated in a story is nonverbal anyway. Bodily and facial expressions can speak as much or more than the words we mouth, and I have found that most of us are far better storytellers than we ever imagined.

There are many ways to approach the following guided fantasies. I have written them to allow you to guide yourself back in memory while you read them. At different points along the way, I'll suggest that you pause and reflect on the suggestions. Take your time. Close your eyes for a moment and see the images that come to mind, feel the sensations that are aroused. Then, read on, resting and closing your eyes at a pace that feels comfortable.

You may find it easier to read through the entire fantasy and then close your eyes, reconstructing the suggested scene in your imagination. Or, if you're meeting with others, select a leader and ask that person to adapt the descriptions and read them while the rest of you close your eyes.

Fire

In sharing this exercise in my workshops over the last few years, I've been privileged to hear hundreds of stories about fire. They seem to come in many shapes and lengths, some heartwarming and others catastrophic. A common theme among men is setting dry fields ablaze or burning garages to the ground while innocently playing with matches. But I've also heard many women tell of their childhood obsessions with fire and how, at the last moment, a watchful parent saved the house from going up in flames. I have also heard countless anecdotes describing the disastrous consequences of pots forgotten on the stove.

But there have been an equal number of stories about camping trips with parents and fond memories of roasting marshmallows. Often, the exercise leads to what amounts to a brief snapshot of a memory, such as that of a child reading into the early morning hours by the light of a single candle. Your stories can be this simple, but you may be surprised by how they still speak in unforeseen ways to those who listen.

THE FIRE FANTASY

Find a comfortable space in which you can relax. Light a candle. If you're with others, place the candle in the middle of your circle. Watch the flame flicker, noticing how it dances in the air. When you're ready, use the candle's flame as a guide back into memory, to an earlier time when something happened in your life with fire. Go with whatever you think of first. *(Pause here for a moment.)*

You'll find that this memory will most probably reveal itself through pictures. Who are the people who are present? What are they wearing? Look around you. What do you see? What do you feel? *(Pause here for a moment.)*

Can you smell the fire's smoke, or hear it as it crackles? Imagine everything that happened, seeing events progress from one scene to another. Take as much time as you need. *(Pause here for a moment.)*

When you have completed your journey with fire, store the scenes in your memory and share the experience with your story circle or with someone who is close to you.

Water

Water, like fire, can alter the course of a life. Without it, we will die of thirst. If there's too much, we can drown. In my own life, water has been the source of pleasure and fun. Waterskiing, sailing, and swimming were important activities throughout my childhood. My mother, though, had a deathly fear that I would drown, and imposed severe restrictions on my involvement with boats. This didn't deter me. With various ironclad alibis, I was able to sneak off with my friends to water-ski at Beer Can Beach.

Many of the stories I have heard from others, though, paint a very different picture. For some, water is the backdrop for significant life passages. I recall the story of one woman who was rowing with her father on a northern lake. He had just opened a small inn that he had built with his life's savings. They saw people on the shore running back and forth from the lake to the inn. As it turned out, they were carrying buckets of water to extinguish the fire that had started in the kitchen. By the time she and her father had returned to the shore, it was too late. Guests had salvaged some of the nicer pieces of furniture, but most of her father's dreams burned to the ground that day. The inn was never rebuilt.

THE WATER FANTASY

Once again, sit comfortably. Imagine that you are lying next to a cool mountain stream. The water cascades over moss-covered rocks, gurgling as it rushes past you. Notice the surrounding trees and the sun's light as it reflects on the shimmering surface of the stream. The sound of rushing water reminds you of days gone by. *(Pause here for a moment.)*

Let the sound of the stream lead you back in your memory, to an earlier time when something happened with water. As with the previous exercise, this memory may come to you in the form of pictures. It may also come in the form of feelings and sensations. There may even be sounds associated with your recollection. Think back on everything that happened. *(Pause here for a moment.)*

Are you alone or are there people involved in what happened? What kinds of feelings come up? Just let the memory wash over and through you. When you have finished remembering everything that happened, return to that mountain stream and once again relax. Hear the bubbling water as it races out of sight. *(Pause here for a moment.)*

Once you are ready, bring your attention back to the present. As with the previous exercise, share with others what happened. Remember to *see* the memory as a movie, simply describing what happened.

Air

When I shared the following fantasy with my teenage stepson, he told me of a dream he had had when he was four years old. He recalled flying through the sky with the freedom of a bird soaring over buildings and treetops. The feeling was so real when he woke that it took days for him to believe he couldn't fly. And now, twelve years later, he still speaks of that time with a question in his voice. Perhaps it really did happen.

THE AIR FANTASY

Imagine that you are standing in an open field. The grass is tall, and the steady breeze makes it ripple like waves on the ocean. Feel the cool wind as it blows through your hair and your shirt. In the sky, a flock of geese glides by and disappears over a stand of trees in the distance. You feel free inside, like the birds as they effortlessly ride on currents of air. *(Pause here for a moment.)*

Think back now on an earlier time in your life when something happened with the wind and the air. Go with whatever first comes to mind. Where are you? What are you doing? Is the wind friendly or dangerous? Is there anyone else with you? How do you feel? Think about everything that happened. *(Pause here for a moment.)*

After you have finished, store your memories in your mind, and return to that open field with the breeze gently blowing the grass. Take a deep breath of the fresh air. See birds in the distance playing in the wind. Imagine how free they feel. *(Pause here for a moment.)*

When you're ready, bring your focus back to the present and share with your family or friends what happened.

Earth

When I think about the earth, my memory returns to the first garden I ever built. I was living in Nashville at the time, and had never grown a vegetable in my life. The backyard of our old house was sunny, so I measured out a plot that was about twenty feet square. Next, I rented a rototiller and spent an afternoon fighting the large rocks buried just beneath the grassy surface and hard clay. After consulting with a friend, I decided that the soil needed aeration, so I hauled in nearly a ton of sand, tilling that in as well. That year we enjoyed some magnificent yellow and zucchini squash, and we had bumper crops of radishes and okra. The real harvest was the joy I experienced in planting the seeds and watching the plants burrow up through the soil, flower, and turn into miracles before my eyes.

Not all experiences with the earth are so enriching. Perhaps you survived an earthquake, or grew up on a farm and lived through a drought or the destruction of all the crops by pestilence. All of these experiences are the fertile ground in which story can take root.

THE EARTH FANTASY

See yourself sitting on a large root with your back firmly supported by the crook of an oak tree's trunk. Thick roots fan out around you, disappearing into the soil. The earth to either side of you is loose and moist from a hard rain just the night before. Take a handful of dirt, bringing it to your nose. The aroma is rich. Examine it closely. What do you see? A muddy trail runs beside where you are sitting. Get up and begin slowly walking. To your left is a boulder the size of a large truck. Climb to the top. Notice that its reflective surface shimmers in the sunlight. *(Pause here for a moment.)*

Think back now to a time when something connected to the earth happened to you. Go with whatever memory comes to mind. How did you feel? Were you safe and secure, or was your life in danger? See the experience in its entirety, from the beginning to end. *(Pause here for a moment.)*

Once you have finished remembering everything there is about that event, store the memory in your mind, and return to the large boulder in the oak forest. Feel the warmth of the rock, heated by the sun, then take a deep breath. *(Pause here for a moment.)*

When you are ready, return your attention to your present surroundings and share the experience.

Defining Moments

There are many words or phrases that can trigger important memories, flooding our imaginations with vivid, colorful pictures and feelings. Sometimes these ideas have a broad cultural significance, referring to a historical incident that shaped all of our lives. Defining moments such as the bombing of Pearl Harbor, the assassination of John Kennedy, and the *Challenger* explosion can indelibly imprint themselves in our memories. Most people alive at those pivotal times could probably tell you specifically where they were and what they were doing. For example, I was an exchange student in Spain at the time of Neil Armstrong's first step from the lunar module. It was the middle of the night, and my Spanish family was riveted by the images on their small black-and-white set. I vaguely recall waiting for hours for Armstrong to take that first step while we listened to Spain's version of Walter Cronkite. The next day my friend Jesús and I were looking up at the moon. With a wide grin he exclaimed, "You Americans are magnificent!" Even though I had nothing to do with this feat, I recall my feelings of self-esteem and self-importance increasing.

There's a lot of rich detail to this memory, but it is filtered through all the subsequent events that have occurred in my life. For example, I'm embarrassed to admit that I may have fallen asleep before Armstrong took that step, but I'm not certain. Since then, I've seen the footage so many times that it has quite naturally been woven into my memory of that evening in Spain over twenty-five years ago. Because memory is both selective and interpretative, my facts may be wanting, but the spirit of the story does capture a proud moment in the life of this country that deeply affected me. To paraphrase a popular saying in the storytelling world, we needn't be burdened about whether every detail of a story is true. Rather, we should be concerned about the *truth* of the story. This story fills that bill for me.

Other pivotal events can affect just a small community. For example, Hurricane Andrew's devastation of Miami or the bombing of the federal building in Oklahoma City had a profound impact on residents in those cities, but for the rest of us who weren't literally or figuratively in the "eye of the storm," these tragedies had little effect. They were but one of many painful headlines at that time, and I doubt that many of us could say where we were or what we were doing when first informed of these tragedies. But these events became life-defining experiences for the people who lived through them.

At a more personal level, most of us who are currently married could probably tell a story about the first time we laid eyes on our spouse. I met my wife on the first night of an interfaith workshop. Nearly fifty people were gathered in the conference facility's lounge. It was crowded, and many of us were sitting on the floor. Next to where I was sitting there was one small space for another person. Late as usual, my future wife slipped into the room and found that space. I noticed that she was attractive, but didn't think anything more about her until the next day. She noticed my name tag and that of my sister-in-law, Linda, who was sitting next to me. Later, I discovered that she thought I was cute but assumed I was married. It puzzled her, though, because in her estimation Linda and I didn't seem to fit together. The rest is history.

When reflecting back on such moments, it's important to think back with an eye toward specifics while also understanding that perception is selective and that memory is ultimately an interpretative process. Even so, it's often our memory of the small details that will reveal important truths about ourselves and the other people in these historical narratives.

The following are offered as historical events worthy of reflection. Some are quite specific, referring to a particular moment in time. Others are more general, pointing to a time that was filled with many exciting and difficult incidents. Not all of them will elicit important memories, but it's probable that a good number will open doors to forgotten and meaningful recollections.

HISTORICAL EVENTS FOR REFLECTION
the stock market crash of 1929
the Great Depression
Pearl Harbor
D-Day
Hiroshima and Nagasaki
the surrender of Japan and Germany in World War II
the Korean War
the Kennedy-Nixon television debate
the Cuban Missile Crisis
Vietnam
the assassination of John Kennedy
the assassination of Robert Kennedy
the assassination of Martin Luther King, Jr.
the 1968 Democratic convention
Kent State
the *Challenger* explosion
the fall of the Berlin Wall
the Gulf War

These are but a few of the defining moments in my life and in the lives of people with whom I have worked. I encourage you to think back in time and add to this list the events that were determining factors in your life. Where were you, and what were you doing when these events occurred?

Archetypal Keys

Many expressions have an archetypal quality, leading us into areas of private experience that may have a universal resonance with the experiences of others. Just a word or phrase can open up a whole vista of memory. This section offers a number of these iconic words for your reflection. I suggest that you simply stop at each and close your eyes for a moment while you reflect on it. If you recall an incident related to the word, take the time to remember everything that happened. As in the above fantasies that focused on the four elements, go with whatever first comes to mind. Think about where you were, what you were doing, if there was anyone else with you, and how you felt. After you have finished, store your memories in your mind, then bring your focus back to the present and share with your family or friends what happened.

WORDS FOR THOUGHT

adventure	camp	first impression
ball game	car accident	flood
beach	country	flying
bicycle	dancing	gift
birthday	doctor	girlfriend
boyfriend	explosion	haircut
broken	failure	hero
brother	fall	hiding place
burnt food	favorite store	holiday meal
business	fire	hurricane

job	political election	summer
lie	rain	swimming
locked out	reading	teacher
lost	relative	travel
math	sailing	tree
mountain	school	trouble
party	sister	vacation
pet	snowstorm	war
picnic	spring	weeping
plane crash	success	winter

This is by no means an exhaustive list. See if you can add to it. Many times, one idea can lead to many memories that result in hours of sharing.

CHAPTER 8

The Memory Walk

Now that you have discovered the ease of recapturing a memory, you are prepared to expand your journey and tackle more challenging and interesting terrain. The following exercises, guided fantasies, and suggestions can aid you in opening up the diverse and rich events that have helped to make you who you are, equipping you, in later chapters, for the more difficult passage into areas of emotional hurt and pain.

Sensing Our Way into the Past

So far, we have focused almost exclusively on the visual nature of memory as a primary medium for recollection. Using the other senses as a path to memory can also produce rich material. The senses of hearing, touch, taste, and smell possess an associative power that can immediately transport us back in time to forgotten places and people.

Aroma Therapy

When I was young, a visit to my grandmother's apartment started when I stepped off the elevator. The hall was filled with the aroma of her cooking. One day, it would be the smell of brisket roasting in the oven. Another day, the overpowering aroma of cakes and cookies would fill my nostrils. Now, whenever I smell Jewish cooking, I'm reminded of her.

Smell can be a powerful stimulator of memories: a grandparent's musty house; marketplaces filled with fresh meats, fish, and vegetables; beauty parlors and barbershops; the scent of a father's cologne or a mother's perfume; the rich aroma of freshly turned earth; a barn; freshly mown grass; coffee percolating; bread baking; a new car; popcorn; mothballs; pine trees; diesel exhaust; and fresh roses.

THE AROMA FANTASY

Each smell can evoke a scene from the past. Sit quietly, take a long, deep breath, then slowly exhale. Imagine that you are in a magical room lined with shelves. On these shelves are bottles filled with every natural and human-made aroma from around the world. Thinking back on the aromas of your childhood, reach for the bottle containing the smell of your parents' kitchen and open it. Take down the bottle containing the aroma of your grandmother's kitchen and do the same. Recall these smells. *(Pause here for a moment.)*

If you had any special chores, were there any strong aromas associated with them, like cutting the grass or cleaning the barn, or feeding coal into a hot furnace? Take the appropriate bottle off the shelf and remove the lid, inhaling deeply. Go with whatever comes to mind. *(Pause here for a moment.)*

Now recall the town you lived in. Were there any strong smells associated with the area, like the pungent stench of a paper mill, or the suffocating reek of car exhaust? Find the bottle filled with these aromas. *(Pause here for a moment.)*

Were there any dominant aromas at the school you attended? Open these bottles as well. *(Pause here for a moment.)*

Think of other important places in your childhood—doctors' offices, gas stations, beauty parlors, locker rooms, or places you worked—and open up the bottles filled with the essence of these places. *(Pause here for a moment.)*

Once you have completely scanned your memory, walk out of your magic room and close the door behind you, returning your attention to the present. If you are sharing stories with others, tell them what you remember, describing in detail the aromas of your childhood.

The Tastes of Childhood

Cooking and eating have always played an important role in my family life. Dinner was usually the one time when everyone was together, for better or worse.

But the significance of food can extend far beyond issues of nourishment or community. Certain dishes can become symbols for love, sibling rivalry, and even humor. Over the years my grandmother, Momo, made a yeast cake that was more like a delicious bread chock full of nuts, cinnamon, and sugar. These cakes were prized possessions in my family, especially after I moved to Orlando, where my brother lived. Every time he and his wife visited my grandmother in Tampa, she entrusted them with a whole yeast cake with directions to share half of it with me. Weeks later I would discover in a casual conversation with her that my brother's family had eaten the whole thing, never mentioning its existence. On the next visit, Momo would scold my brother for his selfishness, entrust him with another yeast cake with clear directions to share it with me, and once again he and his family would eat the whole thing. Now that Momo has died, when we get together we fondly remember her yeast cake and all the mischief and laughter it produced.

THE TASTE FANTASY

Sit comfortably, and imagine a large, warm kitchen. You're sitting at the breakfast table from your childhood. It's covered with dishes of your favorite foods. Everything you used to like as a child is waiting to be eaten. Imagine now all the foods on the table. *(Pause here for a moment.)*

Sample from each one, leaving the desserts for last. When you take the first bite of each, recall when you used to eat each dish. Where were you? Who else joined you? Who did the cooking or baking? How did you feel about this person? What other foods were served? What is your fondest memory of that time? Do this with every food in front of you. *(Pause here for a moment.)*

Every taste carries with it a story. Once you have completed your sampling, imagine that you push yourself away from the table and walk out a swinging back door. Now return your attention to the present. When you are ready, share with others what you recalled.

The Magic of Touch

Babies who are isolated and receive no touch will become developmentally delayed. They can even die. Through touch we discover connection with the world, intimacy, love, and sensual delight. Unlike other sense organs, every inch of our skin is a receptor for sensations from the world. Touch can come in a million forms—the feel of white sand between our toes during a walk on the beach, moist earth rubbed between our fingers, or even the wind blowing briskly on our bare faces. Each of these feelings can lead to wonderful and significant memories.

When I was a child, I couldn't wait for my parents to have a party. All of my mother's friends would wear their mink stoles and chinchilla coats and leave them piled in a heap on my parents' bed. When no one was watching I sneaked in there just to run my hands over the fur. It was a marvelous feeling. To this day I like to touch things that are soft and velvety.

THE TOUCH FANTASY

Imagine lying on a soft blanket under a shady tree. To your side, there is beautiful, thick grass. Let your hands run through it, feeling the cool, pliant blades. A light, warm breeze is blowing. Feel it against your skin. *(Pause here for a moment.)*

Think back now on your earliest memory of being touched by your parents, or touching them. What did that feel like? Do you recall where you were? What were you doing? *(Pause here for a moment.)*

Scanning your childhood memories, think of something you used to touch all the time. What did it feel like? Take a moment to remember everything that occurred then. *(Pause here for a moment.)*

Let your mind wander back in time to other sensations. Scan the different parts of your body, thinking of the different sensations they each feel. Take plenty of time with each one. See where you were, what you were doing, and the other people who were present. Were these feelings pleasurable, neutral, or painful? When you have exhausted all your early memories, see yourself returning to that soft blanket under the shade tree. Take in a deep breath, and relax. *(Pause here for a moment.)*

When you're ready, return your attention to the present and share what you felt and saw

The Sounds of Childhood

Sounds can remind us of many forgotten times. Perhaps there were distinctive noises that were present during your childhood, like trains passing on nearby tracks, airplanes flying overhead, your mother sweeping the front porch, the slamming of your father's car door when he returned home from work, children playing in the neighborhood, the dumping of coal down a chute in the cellar, or the chirping of birds that woke you every morning at dawn.

THE SOUND FANTASY

Sit quietly for a minute or two. Imagine that you are standing in a special room equipped with speakers that surround you with sound. On the walls are audiotapes from every moment of your life, with recordings of all the sounds you have ever heard. There is a comfortable chair in the middle of the room. See yourself sitting down. In the chair is a console that allows you to select any sound for playing. You can control the volume and when to turn the sound on or off. Think back now on an early sound that you used to hear when you were growing up. Play that sound now on your stereo system. *(Pause here for a moment.)*

When you hear the sound, what does it remind you of? Where did the sound occur? Was it made by a person or a machine? Was it friendly or dangerous? How does it make you feel now? Remember everything that occurred in relation to that sound. *(Pause here for a moment.)*

When you have heard enough and remembered everything about that sound, push the button on the console and turn it off. Now think back on other sounds from your childhood. As you recall each one, play it on the stereo system and let your mind drift back to all the memories that occurred in relation to that sound. *(Pause here for a moment.)*

When you have listened to all the sounds that you can remember, get up from the chair and go out of the room. Return your attention to the present and share the sounds of your childhood and the memories they stirred. If you like, try replicating for others what these noises sounded like.

The Music of Our Youth

Every generation has its representative musical sound. For me it was the Beatles and the Rolling Stones. For my brother it was Elvis and Buddy Holly. My dad's generation danced to the tunes of Benny Goodman and the big bands.

When we hear music, especially from the formative times of our lives, there are often experiences and stories associated with those songs. I recall my excitement when my brother brought home the hit record "The Peppermint Twist." This was a treasure that he was kind enough to let me play even when he was out of the house.

Think back now and remember your favorite tunes. If you have them, it often helps to replay those early albums. As you recall the music, picture yourself listening to it. Were you at home or at a dance? What kinds of dreams and fantasies did the music evoke? Were you in love? Did you have your heart broken by someone? Can you recall your school parties? Whom did you go with? Did you dance close? Did you have a radio in your car once you were able to drive? Remember everything that happened.

Commercial radio and television jingles can also be memory markers. Products and their slogans like Lucky Strike cigarettes (L.S.M.F.T.) and Brylcreme ("A little dab'll do you") are indelibly imprinted on each generation's consciousness. Which jingles can you recall? Do you remember how old you were when you first heard them? What associations do you have with these products? Do they bring back any significant memories?

Theater of the Mind

Recalling old radio programs and the colorful personalities behind the microphones can also awaken many forgotten memories. Whenever I speak with elders who grew up during the radio generation, their faces light up with expressions of joy when I ask them about their memories of those early radio shows. Listening was a family event that brought everyone together. In many ways, it was the closest thing to storytelling.

Think back to those old programs. Which ones were your favorites? What about the personalities of the day? Where was your radio? What special things happened before and after the shows? To jog your power of recollection, here are a few names that may bring back fond memories.

Jack Benny   The Lux Radio Theater
The Great Gildersleeve   Your Hit Parade
Walter Winchell   Wolf Man Jack
Ripley's Believe It or Not   Amos 'n Andy
Edward R. Murrow

Movie Memories

Old movies and TV shows can often have the same effect on us as music. Reflect on important movie titles during your youth. If they're available, rent them from your local video store and watch them together as a family. Always leave time at the conclusion to share memories and associations.

There are many movies that can stimulate reminiscing. *It's a Wonderful Life* with Jimmy Stewart can put you in touch with the rich meaning of a simple, well-lived life. Often, good intentions in everyday situations make for more wonderful stories than dramatic events.

Another movie I have used in my storytelling courses is *Avalon*. It traces the lives of five brothers who came to America seeking a dream. It's filled with storytelling as well as a powerful message for all those who want to preserve their family's heritage.

A more recent film, *The Joy Luck Club*, will take you back to the formative relationships in your childhood. In poignant and powerful stories, the lives of four mothers and their daughters are painted in one beautiful scene after another. Each will surely awaken forgotten memories of your own mother, however difficult or harmonious that relationship was.

Movie theaters also hold special memories. The Tampa Theater in the heart of my downtown was a mystical place during my childhood. The ceiling was filled with pin lights that sparkled like stars when the lights were turned down. Faux balconies on the sides gave it a feeling of old Spain. It was here that I first saw *House on the Haunted Hill*, the scariest movie I ever sat through. A large skeleton rigged on a wire floated out over the audience at a crucial moment in the film, and everyone screamed at the tops of their lungs. That night I went into my bathroom to run water in the tub. I was frozen stiff when I went to reach for a washcloth and towel in the cabinet above the toilet. I was certain that the bloody hand that floated out of the vat of acid in the movie was waiting for me there, hovering in preparation to attack and kill me!

"These are a few of my favorite things . . ."

As children, we easily become attached to things like blankets, dolls, stuffed animals, rocks, coins, and special toys. These were our prized possessions that went everywhere we went and were kept in a ceremonial place in our room. How we received these precious gifts and how we lost or damaged them can be a source of important memories. After all, the bond here was as great or greater than the one we had with our parents and other significant people in our lives.

Looking back . . . Did you have a special belonging that was dearer to you than anything in the whole world? What was it? Who gave it to you? Describe it. Was it ever damaged or destroyed? Lost? What happened? How did you feel? Did you share it with other children, or was it something that you played with privately? Can you recall when and where you played with it? When did it cease to be magical? When did you lose interest in it and stop playing with it? Do you still have it?

Time

When we were younger, time seemed so plentiful, stretching forever. A three-month summer vacation was an eternity. The last day of school was like a month. Sometimes, though, we'd become so engrossed in play that we'd lose all sense of time. Before we knew it, our moms would be calling us for dinner.

Looking back . . . Think back on your childhood and remember moments when there was plenty of time. Where were you? Were you on vacation? Was it enjoyable or boring? How did you pass the time? Were there moments when time went slowly and you couldn't wait for something to be over? How did you mark the time then? Did you have a watch? What did it look like? When did you first become aware that time was passing differently? How did it feel? What is your sense of time today?

Nature

Our early experiences in nature can often be pivotal moments in our development. When I was a child, my father would take me and my brother to the beach nearly every Sunday. We'd all pile in the car early in the morning and reach the Gulf of Mexico by nine. On windy days, I can recall trying to walk with my raft as it was nearly swept away. After my sister was born and my brother was getting too old to be seen with kids our age, my dad continued this ritual with Debbie and me until I was nearly twelve.

Looking back . . . The water played an important role in my youth. In yours it might have been the mountains or nearby forests. Think back on your earliest memory of being in nature. Who did you go with? What did you do? Was it something you looked forward to or dreaded? Did you ever go fishing? Hunting? What was it like for you when you caught your first fish? Killed your first animal with a gun? What feelings did it bring up for you? What season was it? Was there anything special that happened once you returned inside? Do you still have any mementos from that time?

Regrets

As children, we often act impetuously, doing things we'd like to take back. When I was five or six and at day camp, I hit a little boy for a reason I can no longer remember. He was wearing glasses, and they broke, cutting his face. As I watched blood stream down his nose, I was shaken and began sobbing uncontrollably. From that day on, I abhorred fighting and rarely got into conflicts, even through my teen years. If I knew how to find that little boy today, I'd go to him and ask for his forgiveness.

Looking back . . . Take a moment to scan your life, starting when you were a child. If it's helpful, work in seven-year increments. During those early childhood days, did you do something to hurt someone, either on purpose or by accident? Did you do it to avenge something he or she had done? Can you recall why you did it? What happened? What happened to the other person? Were there any other repercussions? Were you punished if you were caught? What was the punishment? Did you feel any remorse? What would you say, if anything, to that person today? Would you ask them for forgiveness? Have you forgiven them for anything they did? Have you forgiven yourself? As you scan the rest of your life, repeat this exercise.

Secrets

Our secrets silently speak of the things we hold most dear. The things we conceal can come in so many different forms—feelings of affection and love, knowledge of something important, sacred trusts, hurts, transgressions, and horrible things we have witnessed. When I was young, I somehow learned not to share with my family anything about the young girls I fancied. This pattern continued into my adulthood, and it was not until my mother died that I felt comfortable enough to bring a girl home for the scrutiny of my family. As I think of all the years I spent concealing my feelings in this way, it brings tears to my eyes.

Looking back . . . Scan your life as in the previous exercise, starting at birth and working forward in seven-year increments. What were the secrets you held dearest to your heart? What was the nature of your secrets? Was there anyone in your life you could entrust with these private and precious parts of your self? Why couldn't you share these things with anyone else? What were your most painful secrets? Is there anything you'd want to say to anyone today who hurt you? Do you still feel you can't share these secrets with anyone? Why? Do you have any secrets in your present life? What is the physical, emotional, or spiritual cost of keeping these things hidden? What would be the cost of sharing these with others? What secrets will you take with you to the grave?

Lies and Deception

I grew up with a mother who was rigidly overprotective and constantly worried about my welfare. Whereas most of my friends at age five or six had very liberal boundaries for our biking adventures, I was restricted to a few blocks from the house. I did what any little boy would do whose friends had greater freedom. I disregarded the rules and lied if directly questioned. This pattern continued all the way through high school and even into college, when such questioning became increasingly inappropriate. I think she knew I wasn't being completely straight with her. It was our little game. But I knew she would sleep better at night believing that I was safe and sound.

Looking back . . . What were the small white lies you told as a child? Why did you feel a need to lie? Were you ever caught in the act? What were the consequences? Was the punishment commensurate with the transgression? Was it far worse or far better than you expected? Did you ever go beyond the realm of harmless little lies and tell a blatant lie about something really important? What were you hiding? Were you ever found out? Did you ever tell anyone? How did this affect your relationships? What kinds of lies are you still telling? What feelings or actions do you still feel a need to conceal? What would happen if you came clean and told the truth?

Early Successes

In a culture that is so achievement oriented, it is easy to lose touch with the numerous small successes along our life paths. The proverbial glass can be two-thirds full, but we may have a tendency to disregard all the positives and dwell exclusively on what is absent.

For patients in hospice care, this is painfully the case. When a person is struggling with a life-threatening illness, the tendency is to focus on the failure of the body to ward off the disease. Self-esteem suffers from this narrow viewpoint, often leading to the conclusion that all of life has been a bust. We cannot give these people their health, but what is available is a widened outlook that includes the many successes that preceded the sickness.

Achievements and success produce positive feelings of self-worth. From infancy, each of us has been faced with learning challenges that we have met and joyfully moved beyond. Whether it's a first step on our own, learning to write our name, or riding a bicycle without training wheels, each of these moments was worthy of being celebrated. Retelling the story of these important moments in our growth can literally take us back, body and soul. Remember, the body doesn't know the dif-

ference between a real event and an imagined one. Whether
you're sick or just downhearted, recalling early successes can fill
you with the joy of achievement.

THE SUCCESS FANTASY

Think back to a time when you first did something successfully
that you felt good about. Go with whatever comes to mind. It
needn't be anything spectacular. It can be something as simple
as the first time you dived off the high board or played a short
musical piece from beginning to end without making a mistake.
Remember everything that happened, seeing it like a movie.
(Pause here for a moment.)

Who were the people in your memory? What role did they
play in your success? How did you feel? *(Pause here for a moment.)*

When you have recalled everything you can remember, return your attention to the present and share your memory.

Work

Our first jobs taught us a great deal about the value of hard work.
Lifelong patterns of behavior were often set into motion by
these early experiences.

My earliest recollection of doing chores was weeding flower
beds in our yard. This was the thing I dreaded the most on a
hot, humid Florida day with blood-sucking mosquitos hovering
around my exposed skin. My father subscribed to the pull-
them-out-at-the-root method. This took far too much time, especially if my friend Paul was waiting for me to finish so we could
play. Therefore, I devised the chop-off-their-heads method and
learned to craftily cover up the evidence. When my dad came
home for lunch to inspect the job, I was given a thumbs-up and
was free for the remainder of the day. The only problem was
that the condemning evidence would poke up its nasty head

within a couple days, and my dad would give me a stiff lecture
about the repercussions in life of taking shortcuts.

The lesson stuck, even though I still hate pulling weeds. Only
now, when my wife enlists me for this task, I take them out by
the roots, even feeling a slight sting of remorse if the stem breaks
off above the ground.

Looking back . . . Can you remember your first chores? What
was the first job you had where you earned money? How much?
How many other jobs did you have as a young person? What
did you like most about work? What did you like least? What
kinds of people did you work with? What kind of person was
your boss? Did you like him or her? Thinking back on all these
early work experiences, what is the one thing you learned during this time that carried over into adulthood?

Religion and Spirituality

For me there is a real distinction between religious experience
and spiritual experience. The former occurs in a place of worship and study and, depending upon your upbringing, is filled
with traditions, rituals, liturgy, and a host of other experiences.
The latter may or may not occur in such a place.

Most of the times I have felt deeply connected to God occurred in the wilderness, far away from any sectarian service
filled with moral prescriptions. Once, while sitting beside Thousand Islands Lake on the John Muir Trail in California, I was
filling up our water bottles and preparing to return to the campsite. It was late afternoon, and the Minarets, jagged peaks that
stretch from one horizon to the next, were silhouetted by the
soft glow of the setting sun. Suddenly, the breeze began to blow
in my direction. As it created ripples on the water and rustled
my clothes, I felt a welling up of emotion that was like being filled
with the love of God. Overwhelmed, all I could do was sit and

cry. Never in my life had I experienced anything like it. I was not particularly religious, although I had read mystics' accounts of similar experiences. It took me many years to speak about this ineffable experience with anyone else.

Looking back . . . What was your early religious experience like? While participating in your church, synagogue, or mosque, did you experience God in the midst of all the activities and liturgy? What was that like for you? Did you like these religious settings? Was there anything oppressive? What questions were answered by your clergy? What questions were never answered? Did something that happened there drive you away as a young adult? If you are still active, what things do you fondly look back upon? Did you have a spiritual experience apart from your involvement with your religion? Did you tell anyone about it or keep it private? Was it scary or deeply fulfilling? How did this affect the way you feel about religion, spirituality, and God today?

Celebrations and Rituals

The revelry associated with joyous times is an important beacon as we search for relevant experiences in our past. Celebrations like Christmas and birthdays have their own rhythms that impress on each year a structure and a framework for nearly all of the other events that precede and follow.

In my story "Christmas on Terrace Drive," the energy of the season led me to a significant discovery. As I think back, the Jewish holiday of Passover that celebrates our deliverance from the oppression of slavery in Egypt was also a warm and meaningful time in my childhood. One of the most important events associated with this holiday was the hiding of the *afikomen*, a piece of matzo that must be found by the children before the meal can be finished. Traditionally, the winner receives a handsome prize for his or her efforts. Because this ritual meal was nearly always held at my house, and my parents naively hid the matzo before everyone else arrived, I always had a head start on my cousins. Invariably, I would discover it before they arrived, and nearly always walked away with the reward.

Looking back . . . What kinds of celebrations were important in your home? Were there any special rituals associated with these times? What is your earliest recollection of these events? What was your favorite part? Least favorite? Who led these rituals in your family? Who else was present? What is your fondest memory of these times? How have you continued these traditions in your adult life? What do you miss most as you look back?

Things Lost and Found

Growing up is filled with a series of new experiences and milestones, but also a nearly endless list of things that naturally pass out of our lives. At five, I learned that my mother was pregnant and that I would soon have a new baby sister. This was very exciting. I recall helping my father prepare the baby bed, giving it a fresh coat of paint and adhering a gold star onto its side. Then, one day, I was called to the phone at Helen Hill Kindergarten. My dad was on the other end, letting me know that Mom had given birth to a beautiful baby girl.

In spite of my enthusiasm, when my mother returned home from the hospital, something disquieting had happened in the household. Whereas I had been the center of the universe, I suddenly became what seemed to be an insignificant planet orbiting somewhere in the distant solar system. My mother was in bed recovering from the cesarean birth, exhausted and unavailable, and I felt forgotten. As much as I welcomed my sister, I also resented her. Life in our family was never again the same.

Looking back . . . What things or qualities were lost in your family? Did anything fill the void? Did the birth of a brother or a sister change your sense of belonging? Were there any qualities that you personally lost? When you discovered that tales you had been told to explain phenomena like Santa Claus were untrue, how did that feel? How did it change the way in which you saw your parents and your world? What kinds of things came into your life along the way? As you grew older and bigger, did you excel in a sport or other activity? Did the financial condition of your family radically change during your childhood? How did this affect the mood in your household and your relationships with your parents and siblings?

Adolescence

These are years filled with change and growth, turmoil and difficulty. Few of us had a clear map for how to navigate the rough seas that come with adolescence.

My biggest challenge during this period was forced upon me. My father had been unhappy with the educational system in my hometown and got it into his head that I would get a leg up on everyone if I went off to prep school in New England. One by one, the rejections came in. I'll never forget the day my parents called me at my cousin's house, joyously announcing that I had been accepted at Mount Hermon, in Massachusetts. This was a dark moment in my life. It meant leaving all of my friends and living on my own in a place I had never seen before.

That fall my parents took me to New York City and put me on a bus at the Port Authority. I waved good-bye as they headed off on their first trip to Europe. As I rode through dingy and dirty towns in Connecticut, I felt as if I had been abandoned in an alien world. When I arrived at Mount Hermon, I found that the kids were sophisticated and had experienced things I had only heard about. Even though I was homesick and lonely, I also recognized that this was an important time of my life. People from around the world became my friends, and I was exposed to radical ideas that affected many of my later decisions.

Looking back . . . What do you remember about your adolescence? What were your dreams? Your disappointments? What were the things you loved to do, and what things did you loathe? What choices did you make? How did these affect your life in the years that followed? How did you feel about your parents at this time? How did you rebel? Did you want to have anything to do with them? What were your main interests? How did you spend your free time? Did you have a job? How much money did you earn? What was your biggest worry? Did any books make an impression on you? Which adults or teachers had the biggest impact on you? Who were your closest friends? Did you have any enemies? Were you in love with anyone? How did you explore your sexuality at this time? Did you lose your virginity? What was your deepest hurt?

The Things You Don't Remember

As you proceeded through the above themes, some things that you had completely forgotten about certainly jumped out and touched you. If you're like me, there are some areas of your life that feel like black holes. Whatever was happening then has disappeared, and there seems to be nothing that can be done to retrieve those early memories. For example, I have very few memories of the classic childhood books that most children are exposed to. In fact, I have only one memory of my father reading to me at bedtime. He had chosen *The Adventures of Huckleberry Finn*, and I was completely enthralled by the characters. For some strange reason (that made no sense then), my mother decided that some of the language in the novel was inappropriate for a child my age. Without any real explanation, my father was forbidden to read it to me. I was devastated. Perhaps out of my anger I stopped asking them to read to me. All I know today is that I have no other memories of bedside tales.

Looking back . . . What things do you not remember? Where

have you stumbled when answering the above questions? How far back can you go before your recollection becomes fuzzy and uncertain? What do you think is the significance of the fact that there is a hole in your memory in these areas? Is there someone you know who might know a piece of the missing story? If your parents are still living, ask them about their recollections of these events. (The one caveat is that you must be careful because this is their interpretation of those events. If you don't feel like their version of the story fits your sense of things, take what feels right and discard the rest.) If you have no stories for a particular area of your life, imagine what happened. What kind of story would you tell? Even though the facts of this fantasy are probably nowhere near the *truth* of what happened, there may be a lot of current truth in your tale just by the fact that you have projected yourself and all of your issues and unresolved conflicts into the heart of the story. If you're still unsure of how to bring your creative imagination to your stories, we'll look at this issue more closely in chapter 14, The Healing Path.

CHAPTER 9

Highs and Lows

Within each family, significant events irrevocably affect and shape the lives of every member. These pivotal times often set into motion powerful forces that reverberate for years to come. In the following sections, I invite you to explore with fresh eyes these central motifs.

Births

I have heard it said that the most important story of our life is about our birth. Children are hungry for details of this event in which they were the central player, but for which they have no memory. They can only learn about the drama of this event through the eyes of others. What they hear will tell them much more than the details of a baby being born. Through this story they learn whether they were welcomed, where they belonged, and if they were loved. For example, I was a premature and cesarean baby. I also know that of three I was the only child who was planned. I'm unsure as to why my parents shared this with

me, but it meant a lot to me as a kid knowing that they had in-
tended for me to be here.

Looking back . . . Do you know the details of your birth? Were
you wanted or were you conceived accidentally? How did your
parents feel about you coming into the family? Were they excited, hopeful, and happy, or did they have reservations? What
time of day were you born? Were there any complications?
Were there any surprises before or after your birth? Was your
father present in the delivery room? How was your name chosen? Do you know what it means? If you had siblings, what was
their reaction to your arrival? What special rituals took place to
honor your birth?

Deaths

The death of family members and even pets can create currents
of sadness and grief that in our society frequently go unexpressed. As children, the meaning of these transitions is usually
not apparent at the time. The finality of death is a difficult con-
cept even for us as adults. But locked within these losses is a
piece of ourselves that can only be retrieved through the telling
of the story.

Morris, my father's father, died when I was seven. This was
a man whom I didn't know well, but I had fond feelings for him.
Whenever he visited from St. Louis, he'd pick me up in his giant
hands. The night my father returned from the funeral, I sat in
his lap as he shared all that had occurred, and I was told that
Grandpa had died of a heart attack. Years later, though, I discovered that this was a story fabricated to protect the children.

I had moved to Chicago to go to school and was staying tem-
porarily with my uncle. While attending a softball game with my
cousin, we were reminiscing about Morris. She casually mentioned that he had committed suicide. In fact, he had hanged

himself while visiting them in Chicago in the very room in which I was staying. This revelation hit me like a bomb.

It took me many years to muster the courage to speak with my father about the real story of Morris's death. When asked about why we were told the story about Morris's heart attack, he was surprised. He didn't even remember it. The real tragedy was that no one really knew why Morris took his life. My father had no clue except to say that in retirement Morris found no reason to go on. It will forever remain a mystery that still touches me deeply.

Looking back . . . Who died in your family when you were growing up? Did a pet die? What were you told about the death? Was the meaning of death explained to you? How was this person important to you? If you went to the funeral, what was it like? Was the body on display? How did you feel? For how long did you grieve? What stories do you remember about this person? What don't you recall? Do you do anything today to keep the person's memory alive?

Sickness

Illnesses can have as much impact on a family as a death, especially if they are protracted. For a child, they can reveal a parent's mortality and fallibility. Sickness can also alter the entire balance of power in a family, profoundly affecting each person's roles and responsibilities.

When I was young, nearly everything in our family revolved around my grandfather George because of his poor health. He had moved from Ohio to Florida after a series of heart attacks led his doctor to advise that the warmer weather would improve his chances of survival. It seems that most of my memories are of him convalescing in the small apartment he shared with my grandmother. We had to be very quiet when we visited. But, when he was feeling strong, he'd return to work.

On Sundays, my grandparents, uncle and aunt and cousins, and our whole family would pile into two cars and take the forty-five-minute drive across the causeway to Wolfie's restaurant in St. Petersburg. I hated those trips and especially disliked the beets and sauerkraut that were served family-style on the large tables. But this was heaven for George. There was nothing better than being surrounded by his family and eating a pastrami on rye sandwich.

Looking back . . . When were you sick as a child? What diseases did you have? The measles? The mumps? Did you ever have your tonsils taken out? Were there any other occasions when you were so sick that you had to be hospitalized? Who cared for you when you were home? Were there any bright spots during this time? How much school did you miss? Was anyone else in your family sick? What happened to them? Was it a long illness? How did their sicknesses affect your life? Did you have to get a job to help out your family? What other decisions in your life were affected by this illness?

Accidents

So many things are out of our control. It's the unplanned-for events that frequently have the biggest impact on our lives. Sometimes accidents have a silver lining, and the outcome is far from what we would have anticipated.

In February 1990, I sold my business and was given a contract to continue working for the company. By June, I was ready to leave but wasn't sure of my direction. One thing was certain: I was going to approach the new tasks with the same style of overworking that had helped me succeed in the past. The events of June twenty-seventh changed all that. While playing golf, I jumped across a large ditch to retrieve my ball. In the process, my left Achilles tendon ruptured so severely that it required surgery. On July second, I returned home from the operating room with a cast up to my thigh. Never before had I been incapacitated like this. In the house, a wheelchair was my only means of self-sufficiency. Just a few days previously I had been the president of a very successful advertising firm. Now I had been stripped of all my titles, and my identity, and I was an invalid.

Without a doubt this was the most difficult challenge I had ever faced, and I couldn't rely on any of my old strategies or coping mechanisms. The frustration of setting a table would bring tears to my eyes. Once I could get around on crutches, everyone I saw seemed to know their place in the world and where they were going, except for me. I was lost.

Through the support of my fiancée and my many friends, I learned about humility and gratitude. I think I'm a better person for it. More important, in those quiet times, my life's vision began to take shape, and my work with storytelling probably wouldn't have come about if it hadn't been for the accident. From the tragedies and difficulties in our lives we can learn many lessons.

Looking back . . . What kinds of accidents did you have as a child? Were you seriously hurt? How were mishaps handled in your family? Were people calm, or did they become hysterical? Did anyone else in your family have an accident? What happened? Was anyone prone to accidents all the time? Did anything bad happen that ended up having a positive outcome? How have you and your family been affected by these accidents?

Coincidences and Good Fortune

Coincidences and fortunate occurrences are close cousins to accidents. Serendipitously we find ourselves in the right place at the right time, and things are never the same.

A few years ago, I was returning from Wyoming, where I had

been backpacking, when I found myself seated next to a couple who also happened to be hikers. There wasn't a mountain trail west of the Mississippi that we didn't talk about. Out of the blue, Carol and Neal asked me if I had ever been to the National Storytelling Festival. I had never heard of such a thing, nor did I know that there were people who told stories for a living. My curiosity was stirred. When they invited me to accompany them to the festival a few weeks later, I jumped at the opportunity. As a result of my first exposure to storytelling, I knew that I would be devoting the rest of my life to the art. If I hadn't met Carol and Neal, who knows where I would be today? Most certainly, I wouldn't be sitting here before the computer writing a book about healing and storytelling!

Looking back . . . What coincidences or lucky breaks happened in your life? What were the unexpected consequences? How did these events influence you? Where do you think you would be now if they hadn't happened? Did such events feel like they were guided by a force or power rather than by a roll of the dice? Do you see these special times differently today than you did when they occurred? Do you feel you have had a lot of good fortune in your life? Bad fortune? How do you see this?

Miracles and Magic

My best friend, Philip, refers to God as the Great Magician. At any moment in time, magic can happen, miraculously transforming situations and people's lives. That's how God works, but the Great Magician is often unpredictable. For years, Philip has been trying to decipher the universal code that governs miracles. Certainly there must be some attitude or behavior that predisposes the Magician to intercede on our behalf.

On one occasion, Philip's favorite cat, Max, disappeared. Every day for weeks he called the Humane Society and the pound hoping that Max would show up. He posted signs throughout his neighborhood advertising a reward for his return. Even though he never lost hope, he also knew he'd be moving soon. Time was running out.

One afternoon, he was talking with a friend about human intention and the process of magic. Innocently, he said to the universe, "If you really want to blow my mind, bring Max back." That afternoon his phone rang. Someone two blocks away had found a cat who was hurt and malnourished. He resembled the description of Max, but he was so filthy the caller couldn't be sure. It was Max. He was nearly half dead, but he was back.

Looking back . . . Did anything magical or mysterious ever happen in your life? At the time, what did you think of these events? How did you explain them? Were other people affected as you were? Whom did the Great Magician use to help bring about this miracle? How is this event still affecting your life? How did it change you? Did it alter your belief system? As a result, are you a different person today?

Turning Points

As we look back, many turning points were painful and difficult to accept. But with hindsight we can sometimes see how what we thought was bad at the time turned out to be good, and what we thought was a curse resulted in a blessing. Sharing this perspective can help us tie up the loose ends of our lives and teach important lessons to younger generations.

Wonderful experiences can also change the course of our lives. It might be the landing of an important job, a new friend who taught you a crucial lesson in living, a handsome boy who asked you to marry him, a day in school, a kiss, or the birth of a child.

Likewise, sometimes good things in our lives are born out of bad experiences. Losing a job can seem like the end of the world at first, but can often be the prod to get you to seek more fulfilling work. Or, a difficult divorce could have taught you a painful lesson that better prepared you to succeed in your next marriage. Even the tragic loss of a child or a spouse can, with time, be a force for healing in our lives.

Looking back . . . What were the important events in your life? Were they painful or pleasurable? At the time, did good things or bad things result? With the passing of time, how did your assessment change?

Did you ever lose a job? Out of the breakups of marriages and other relationships, what happened? What other losses led to a transformation of your life?

The Loss of Innocence

When the fairy-tale quality of life is stripped away, revealing a harsher reality, we must painfully adapt and grow. These eye-openers can come in so many forms: people not always being kind and generous; bad things happening to those we love; wealth evaporating because of others' incompetence; our best friend betraying us; the realization that love is not always forever; our parents choosing to divorce; the knowledge that we are mortal. These awakenings and realizations can thrust us into emotional disarray. Sometimes it can take us months and even years to recover.

When I was in college, I fell in love with my roommate's girlfriend. It was a foolish thing to do. Over the course of that year, I became her confidant, listening for countless hours about how unhappy she was in this relationship. During the summer between our sophomore and junior years, we corresponded weekly, expressing our feelings for each other, and making plans for being together in the fall. When I returned, though, she reneged, feeling guilty and responsible for her boyfriend's fragile mental health. She simply couldn't face him with the truth. I was devastated.

Looking back . . . In what ways were you devastated by your loss of innocence? When do you recall being betrayed by someone for the first time? What time-honored beliefs have you had to give up? When did you first become aware of your mortality? When did you become aware that your parents were not perfect? That being good did not always guarantee that the world would respond in kind? How have you been able to retain your sense of wonder and innocence in the face of all the losses in your life? How have you become jaded and cynical?

The highs and lows of our lives are identifiable signposts for the journeys into our pasts. They help to organize life experiences into coherent and understandable narratives. But frequently, seemingly insignificant things and events can reveal deep and important meanings. In chapter 10, we will look at the ordinary places in our lives that were the backgrounds for our formative childhood years. These walls and rooms can say a great deal about our joys, pains, disappointments, triumphs, and our most troubling wounds.

Places I Remember

I'm not sure it's possible to think of our life stories without considering the places where these small and large dramas occurred. The spaces in our past are filled with power and, sometimes, mystery. They are also a key to helping us identify forgotten memories that can lend meaning and continuity to our life's story. In the following exercises, you'll have an opportunity to revisit these locations and see with new eyes the architecture of your past.

Home

For a child, home is the world. Everything revolves around it. It's the place where formative experiences happen daily. Lifetime patterns of behavior are set into motion here. Most of our childhood hurts and joys occur within the confines of these walls. Enduring relationships with parents and siblings are rooted in the early years. It's no wonder, then, that when we return to our childhood homes as we imagine and remember them, many of the significant events of our childhoods can be released into awareness.

When I was first introduced to these ideas a number of years ago by Sam Keen, I recalled a very important feature of my bedroom. It was the trophy case hanging by the door. My brother, Steve, had built it in shop at junior high, and it was filled with his many tennis and bowling awards. Steve was seven years older, and I can't even count the number of times I had to pass by that case and be reminded of his athletic superiority. Even though I played tennis and pursued other athletic endeavors, deep down, I didn't believe I would be able to compete with him on those playing fields. I skipped from sport to sport, never excelling in anything.

As you follow the directions in the upcoming exercises, look for the things that really meant something, along with the significant events that involved people who lived with you. For me, that trophy case was much more than wooden shelves. So it is with a home that's filled with drywall and sticks of wood and fabric that we call furniture.

The House Plan

Take a piece of blank paper and a pencil and draw the floor plan of the house you grew up in. Remember that this is not a drawing contest, nor are you expected to be a great architect. In fact, it's probable that the proportions of your plan will be off-kilter. It doesn't matter.

Using this exercise, in working with many people, I have found that many of us moved around a great deal during childhood. If that's true for you or anyone else participating in this exercise, choose a house that you remember best before the age of ten. If you're still having trouble recalling the details of an early house, it's okay. I suggest that you draw the floor plan of the home you remember best from your early teen or young adult years.

To draw a floor plan, see the house as though you are looking down from above. Remember to indicate where major furniture is placed in the rooms, the location of windows and doors, and important features of the yard, such as a large tree. If the house is two or more stories, draw each floor separately. Or, if it's an apartment, include external features of the building, such as a playground or courtyard or any other areas where you spent a good deal of time.

While drawing, memories of things that happened will spontaneously come to mind. Jot down a note on the side to remind yourself of the incident or story. For example, if you suddenly recalled the time you dumped a bucket of cold water on your brother from the second-floor window, you could write something as simple as "Cold water on Steve."

Be sure to include any places that were secret. Take note of the rooms you can't remember. Were any of these off-limits to the children in the house? Give special attention to your bedroom.

You will remember numerous stories. Some will be humorous, while others may be sad or even painful. You're in complete control of the exercise. If an area of the house brings up painful memories, you have complete permission not to go there. It's quite normal to shy away from remembering the bad times. Perhaps you'd like to visit that room privately but don't wish to speak about it publicly. That's okay. It's my experience, though, that by sharing such stories we can heal the pain of old emotional wounds and help other family members understand the experiences that shaped our personalities and choices in life.

Take as much time as you need to finish your floor plan. If you are meeting with others, give them a minimum of ten minutes. When everyone is finished, ask whoever is ready to go first and give the rest of the group a guided tour of his house. (Do the same with all the following exercises.) Have him tell at least one story about something that happened. A good story may be as simple as a description of a typical morning on a farm. Others may be filled with drama, pain, and tears. They are all interesting and important.

House Tour Variations

Most of us lived in more than one house as children. Or, you may have spent much of your free time at a grandparent's house while on vacation, or at a friend's house because being in your own house was painful, if not dangerous. Think of all the houses you have lived in and repeat the above exercise for each one. Remember to draw in all the significant features, including furniture. Even though you can't see the walls from above, indicate noteworthy items such as paintings or plaques.

You may find it difficult to recall important details, and may even find yourself confusing the features of one house with those of another. Do the best you can and don't become overly concerned with correctness. The fact that this happens is notable in itself, and it may tell you more about your childhood than the actual contents of any particular home.

Your Neighborhood

Think back on the neighborhood in which you grew up. If you lived in a house, who lived on either side of you? If your parents rented an apartment, did you know the people who lived on your floor? How about on the other floors of the building? Draw a diagram of your neighborhood or apartment building. Indicate where all the houses were and any geographic features such as streams, stands of trees, fields, et cetera. Label each house with the names of all the people who lived there. Include as many streets as you want. For some of you, the neighborhood may be just one block. For others it may encompass much more. Where did you play? Who were your friends? Which houses did you play at most? Which of the adults were nice and which did you avoid? Which yards did you cut through? Was your school nearby, or did you have to ride your bike or take the bus to get there? How was your neighborhood different at night? Was it safe? What are your fondest memories of the place? Your most painful recollections? Of all these people, how many of them do you still know? (Repeat this exercise for all the neighborhoods in which you lived as a child.)

Your School

Think back on the earliest school you can remember. Do you recall your kindergarten or nursery? How about your elementary school? For each of the schools you attended through senior high, draw a rough plan of the school and where your classrooms were. If you can recall some of the actual classrooms, draw these as well on separate pieces of paper. Show the rest rooms and the principal's office. Was there a nurse's station? Did the janitor have a small office? If there was a playground, diagram all the important areas. See if you can remember the name of each teacher, along with the names of the kids in each class. As you are drawing, make notes of the things you remember.

Places of Revelation

Were there any places that were filled with magic or were special retreats that you visited often as a child? As an adult? If so, think about these places and see if you can draw them. If they were natural settings, do your best to show all of the central features, from trees to caves to mountains. After you have finished drawing, describe the things that happened there and what it felt like for you. Share with others these places and their meaning for you.

Your Town

Remember the town in which you grew up. Draw the features of the town that you recall the most. For example, if I was drawing my hometown, I'd show the coin shop and the Tampa Theater in the downtown area, the swamp two blocks from my house, Rocky Point and Palma Ceia golf courses, Mitchell Elementary School, the drugstore on Howard Avenue, my grandparents' apartment building on the bay, Davis Island Tennis Courts, et cetera. Remember, this is not an exercise in cartography. Put your house in the middle of the page and surround it with all these places without worrying about the scale and proportions. You can indicate them by a descriptive phrase or name, or draw them as they looked.

This was your world. How many of these places could you reach by foot? By bike? How else did you get around? Did you rely on your parents to carpool you, or did you ever take the bus? As you survey this wider landscape, what things do you remember? What kinds of adventures did you have? Which places did you want to avoid?

Going Home

Even though home can never be the same for us once we become adults, physically revisiting the places of our youth can take us back in ways that drawing cannot. For example, when I revisited my boarding school in New England a few years ago, the smell of the place, the dandelions in the grass, and the texture of the red brick on the buildings all helped me vividly re-create my years there. These were details I might have overlooked had I just been reminiscing.

When you return home, you'll also be surprised by how small things look. When you're only two or three feet tall, everything is proportionately bigger. You may also be shocked to find that things you thought were wondrous are quite ordinary as you look at them now. But don't let your current perceptions drown out the memory of what it was like as a child. By telling the story again as you recall it, you can imbue the things and people of your childhood with magic and mystery.

Our stories are always made up of places and people. They're inextricably wrapped together. If you are like me when I revisit old haunts and magic spaces, the people from my past practically come to life in my imagination like actors on a stage. In chapter 11 we'll examine who these characters are and the many gifts and lessons we received from them.

Special People and Forgotten Gifts

At times we may feel lonely, but none of us was ever born alone. Even in a cold surgical suite, we were welcomed, at the very least, by nurses, doctors, and our mothers. For many of us our fathers, grandparents, and other relatives were waiting in an adjacent room, prepared to coo and marvel at our emergence on the scene. The moment we were brought home, our world expanded. Brothers and sisters became actors in our drama. Friends, neighbors, and teachers soon entered onto the stage.

This circle can widen and contract throughout our life. Friends of mine, Hedy and Yumi Schleifer, are citizens of the world, with intimate friendships that span continents. Their lives are rich, and the stories they tell are vivid and full of enticing detail and worldly characters who speak dozens of languages. But narrow circles don't always create narrow people. Taking the time to become rooted in a place and intimate with all of the characters there can produce meaningful lives that are brimming with stories. When I first heard Michael Cotter, a third-generation farmer from Minnesota, tell stories about his family's land, I saw in the details of his life a universe that was also bountiful and exciting.

In this chapter, we will explore how the various people in our lives contributed to the creation of who we are. We'll identify the angels along with the villains, the bitter folks and those with hearts of gold, and the ancient ones who are all but forgotten.

Our People

Each of us needs to feel like we belong. We discover ourselves only in relation to others. The primary locus of belonging in our culture is the nuclear family. It's here where we learned our worldview and developed patterns of thinking and behavior that will follow us throughout our lives. But the nuclear family is only a small thread of a much larger fabric.

In this country, few of us can go beyond three generations in the past before we discover that we don't even know the names of our great-grandparents, where they came from, what their struggles were, what their triumphs were, and what their contributions were to this crazy world. We must discover who our people are in order to find out where we belong in the bigger picture. As author Paula Underwood says, we must establish our "pathness" before we can truly engage the future.

Looking back . . . Who are your people? With which cultural and ethnic groups do you identify? What do you know about each of these groups? Where are you ignorant? How many generations back can you go? What remnants of stories do you have about these distant relatives? Do you have any pictures of them? If so, look at the photos. What do you see in their faces? Without really knowing them, what kinds of burdens would you say they are carrying? How do you see yourself in them? Did their professions have any resemblance to your personal or professional pursuits today? If you have few answers to these questions, research your past. Find out where your people came from and why they decided to leave their countries to come to a new world. Adopt the larger cultural story as your own. See how it feels. Try it on for a while.

For example, if you are of Russian origin and your ancestors were peasants, imagine yourself to be living an impoverished life. Imagine your dreams of a better world. Imagine what it would have been like to emigrate to the United States. How would you have gotten to a port? What would you have sold to get there? Whom would you have left behind? What difficulties would you have had to face when you arrived? How would the experience change you?

These are but a few of the ways in which you can enter into the past to discover your path and ancestry. Live and breathe as though you were these people and you will discover who you are and where you belong.

Family Mores and Personalities

The way things were done in our childhood families becomes part of the underlying assumptions that guide us when we go out in the world and create our own families. Luckily for us, none of these things are ever set in stone. We can consciously choose whether to continue these habits, patterns, and beliefs. But first we must see that they are not the way the world has to be, but just one of many ways.

I have a friend whose husband grew up with dogs. Large dogs, to be exact. When he got married, one of the first things on his agenda was to get a large dog. The notion of family and marriage was totally wrapped up with this idea. His wife, unfortunately, didn't grow up with the same experience. So they compromised and got a nice, small dog with a big heart.

Looking back . . . How did your family do things differently than other families you knew? Did you ever question why? If so, what kinds of answers did you get? Did you have any family customs, like a special meal on a particular night? How did this come about? Were there any forbidden topics of conversation? Were there any skeletons in the closet that were discussed behind closed doors or that couldn't be mentioned in public? What were the taboos in your family? The rules? Were these inviolable? What were the consequences of breaking the rules? Were there any sayings that were popular in your family? Was there anything told to you as a child that has stuck with you throughout your life? Were there any family heirlooms that had a story behind them? What were the sentimental objects in your family? Do you know what made them so? How did your parents celebrate? Did they like parties? Picnics? Trips? Which people did you like in your family? Detest? Distrust? Idolize?

Childhood Friends

Paul McCloskey, Jody Savarese, and Eddie Smoak were my partners in adventure, mischief, and creative enterprise. A day hardly went by when we weren't doing something together, and nights were filled with games like Kick the Can underneath the streetlight. Once we spent every spare moment for weeks building a go-cart from all the spare scraps and parts we could find in each other's garages.

These were my best friends, but we were also capable of inflicting great hurt upon each other. Once, these guys decided to toss oranges and grapefruit at me. I just stood there, dodging the fruit, hating being picked on and ostracized for no reason at all. When I could take it no more, I ran home in tears.

The friendships we make in childhood are unlike any others that we develop when we become adults. Next to our parents and siblings, they may have been the most significant relationships we have had.

Looking back . . . Who were your best friends as a child? What were their names? Where did they live? How often did you get together? Did you go to their houses or did they come to yours? What was your favorite thing to do? Think of all the ways in which you used to play. Did you have some friends with whom you did only certain things together? Did you ever hurt each other? What happened? When did you stop being friends? Was there a reason? Did your parents ever try to influence who your friends were? Did you and your friends ever get into trouble? Were you punished? Who was your very best friend? With what kinds of things did you entrust this person? What kind of friend was this person? How long has it been since you last saw these people?

Teachers

Teachers are powerful individuals. Some of mine were so large that just their size could intimidate me. Mrs. Stephens, my sixth-grade teacher, was like a battleship. She wore laced-up black shoes with thick heels, and rarely smiled. Her reputation for stern discipline preceded her. For five years, I dreaded the possibility of being placed in her class, but fortunately, she liked me and we got on quite well that year.

In addition to being powerful, teachers are also influential. When we were young, teachers who cared could make a big difference in our lives. In first grade, Mrs. Bodo believed in me. Because of that I learned to believe in myself. In fourth grade, Mrs. Hood heaped all kinds of classroom responsibilities on me, teaching me that there was rarely anything I couldn't do.

Looking back . . . What kinds of teachers did you have? Can you recall them? Which ones were kind and which ones were mean? Which ones really taught you something? Did a teacher take you under his or her wing, making you feel special? What things do you recall about each class? Do any stories stand out? What lessons from these early years do you remember? What things did you like about each of these people? Dislike? If you

had the chance to go back in time and say anything you wanted
to any of these people, what would you say?

The People We've Admired
and Imitated

Ask anyone whom she or he admires and why, and you will discover more about that person than you can imagine. This answer
will reflect core values and beliefs and will tell you a great deal
about how this person feels about himself and his accomplishments in life. For most of us, this short list changes with time.

As a kid I thought Mickey Mantle, Arnold Palmer, and Johnny
Unitas were the most incredible people on the face of this
planet. By the time I reached my teens, I had read the autobiography of Mahatma Gandhi, and suddenly I had a new hero.
In my early twenties, I became interested in art and found an
example of how I wanted to be in the life of Alexander Calder.
Even as an old man he knew how to play and live imaginatively.
This was a trait that was being squeezed from my life, and I desperately wanted to preserve it. Today, my list still includes
Arnold Palmer, along with many people whose spiritual achievements impress me.

Looking back . . . Whom did you admire as a child? Did you
know them personally, or were they some sort of celebrity?
Make a list of all the people you admired. If it helps, divide your
life into seven-year increments. What was it about each of these
people that made them special? What things did they each do
that impressed you? How were they different from the rest of
the people you knew? Did they ever do something that soured
your view of them? When did they fall from your list? As new
people were added, how did you become aware of them? If you
had a chance to say one thing to one of these persons, what
would it be?

Was there anyone whom you tried to imitate? What behaviors did you mimic? Did you consciously practice to be like them, or did it just seep into your actions? Which of these behaviors is still part of your personality?

Villains and Enemies

As children, we often see people as awful and evil and out to get us. At times their behavior is a response to our own actions, but rarely do we see our contribution to the matter.

When I was in seventh grade I had a chemistry teacher, Mr. Jeffers. He was strict and tough. Everyone knew that they didn't want to cross his path. Once, a few of us came to the lab early and were playing tag between the counters. Unfortunately, I didn't see Mr. Jeffers come in. He moved swiftly down the aisle, grabbed my jacket lapels, and pinned me against the wall. My feet were dangling off the ground as I shook all over. "If I ever catch you fooling around in my lab again, I'll put your head through the wall! Do you understand me?" I was too shaken to answer. All I could muster was a short nod.

From that day on, I feared Mr. Jeffers. Ironically, almost thirty years later I was at a storytelling festival. A man there looked very familiar. His name tag had "Jeffers" written on it. I introduced myself and asked if he had ever taught chemistry in high school. Sure enough, it was him! But he couldn't remember me to save his life, nor could he recall the incident in the lab that is indelibly imprinted on my memory. To my surprise, he's a decent fellow, and we've even grown to be friends over the last few years.

Looking back . . . Who were the people you feared and hated as a child? What did they do to earn this distinction? Did you feel this way about them because of direct experience or because of something someone else had said about them? How did they affect your life? Could you avoid them, or were you forced to interact with them regularly? Was there anything redeeming about them? How has your view of them changed over the years? Do you still know them?

Messengers of Kindness

From time to time, people come into our lives whose very presence often leaves us a better person. These gifts are large and small. They teach us important lessons that continue to guide us. They also can leave us feeling wanted and important. Messengers of kindness can come in many forms: a neighbor who always had milk and cookies waiting whenever we visited; a stranger who took the time to give us a ride home while reminding us to never again take a ride from someone whom we don't know; an uncle who took us on field trips and taught us everything we know about the woods and nature; an aunt who was willing to sit through a double-feature movie on Saturday when no other adult would even consider it.

I have had many such people in my life. One friend, Louise Franklin Sheehy, has not only encouraged me every step of the way in my career as a storyteller, but through her recommendation this book was considered for publication. The last five years would look very different if she hadn't been in my world.

Looking back . . . Draw a time line starting at zero, with hash marks to represent every seven-year segment of your life (0, 7, 14, 21, et cetera). During each time period, identify someone who was a messenger of kindness. Their contribution needn't be something monumental. It could be someone who set an example, helped you with a chore, was a special love, or someone who always took the time to notice you and smile. Write the person's name beside that period along with the thing he or she did. You may find there are some periods where you draw a blank. That's okay. Just skip that period and move on to the next.

When you're done, choose one of your messengers and tell

another person everything you can remember about him or her. It's often helpful to have the listener ask questions, probing for details that may illuminate the role the messenger played in your life. What was the gift you received? How did it affect your life? How have you become like the person who paid you an act of kindness? Have you ever given this kind of gift to another person?

An essential part of any important relationship is the emotional connection. Whether the feelings are positive or negative, they are a powerful link to our past and may still be coloring the way we see ourselves and others. In the next chapter, we will use the dynamic world of our emotions to gain access to and understand the past and the present.

CHAPTER 12

Emotional Connections

If there is one constant in our lives, it's our emotions. We can't be in this world without feeling something. For many of us, there are dominant emotions that show up again and again. A person with a hot temper can trace back through her life and mark the calamitous times when anger got the better of her. If sadness has been a pervasive theme, despairing moments will be as apparent as dead patches of grass in a lush, green field.

In this chapter, we will use our emotions as guides back in time to recover memories that may have fallen through the cracks in earlier exercises. I'll ask you to experience each of these feelings, and even befriend the more difficult ones. I hope that out of this process you will discover parts of yourself that have been walled in by judgment or self-pity.

Anger

Anger was never an easy feeling to express in my household. I can hardly recall anyone ever raising his or her voice or lashing out, except once. My brother had just bought a fake ink-spill trick. It came with a piece of metal in the shape of a small pool of ink that was painted a glossy black. There was also an empty ink bottle. My mother had just had the indoor planters covered over with slabs of expensive marble. It was her pride and joy.

On this particular day, we set up the fake ink spill on the marble's surface and waited for her to come home. I was beside myself with anticipation. When I heard her come in the kitchen door, I couldn't restrain myself and stuck my head around the corner to see the expression on her face. What happened was much more than I ever expected.

As she rounded the bend into the dining room and saw the ink, I was bursting with laughter. She was enraged and began screaming and pummeling me. Our joke suddenly turned into a horror film. I don't know how long the beating lasted. It seemed to go on forever. When my brother interceded, she stopped and left me there crying. I imagine that she was both furious and ashamed. That was the first and last time my mother ever hit me, but we never spoke another word about the incident.

Looking back . . . Think back on the times in your childhood when you were angry. What happened? Did anyone do something to hurt you? Were you physically harmed, or was it just your dignity that got bruised? How did you handle your anger? Did you throw temper tantrums or did you quietly steam and simmer? How did people react when you became angry? Was it safe to express your feelings, or dangerous?

Were there people in your family who often became angry? How did they express it? What kind of effect did this have on you? Were you ever hit? Or did the person wait for the anger to subside before reacting to you?

How is anger a part of your life today? Have you continued from childhood the same pattern of dealing with your anger, or has it changed?

Love

There are so many different kinds of love—filial, parental, platonic, and romantic. Parental love I took for granted. It was hard, though, to say that I loved my siblings. Other emotions ruled the day in these relationships. I discovered romantic love very early on. After age six, hardly a month went by that I didn't have a crush on a girl at school. I recall at elementary school walking up the stairs behind Cindy Sawyer, mesmerized by the way her blond hair fell into two large curls on her neck. She was the most beautiful girl I knew, but I hardly felt worthy enough to say anything to her, much less express how I felt.

Looking back . . . Who were the people you loved as a child? Where did you meet? What was it like for you? How did it make you feel? If you fell in love with someone, did they reciprocate? How did you express your affection? Did you give each other anything as a symbol of that affection, like a ring or a pin? Can you recall your first kiss? What was it like? What did you like most about this person? Least? If you broke up, who initiated it? Where and how did you break up? How did you meet your next boyfriend or girlfriend?

What other kinds of love did you experience? How did you know that your parents loved you? Your siblings? Your relatives? Your friends? Did you ever have a friend whom you loved? Did you ever express it?

Hate

Hate, like love, can be all-consuming. We can spend our lives hating someone, at great cost to our physical and emotional health, without it having an iota of impact on that person. Hate can also be fleeting. A child can love his best friend in one moment, hate her in the next, and by tomorrow be best friends once again. Hate is also confusing and difficult to express. In our culture, it's not nice to hate someone. It's practically a taboo. For most of us, hate is a private affair that we can only discuss in our most intimate relationships. For others, it's a public event mixed with vitriolic anger, as in the case of skinheads and neo-Nazi youth.

Looking back . . . Whom did you hate as a child? Why? How did you act out your hatred? How did you keep your hatred private? When you think of that person today, do you still feel spiteful? What happened, if anything, to resolve these feelings? Was it satisfying?

Did anyone ever hate you? Why? What did they do about it? Did they ever express it to you? How did it make you feel? Did you react with anger or hatred yourself, or were you able to take more constructive action?

Envy and Jealousy

At the end of my street there lived an elderly couple who became guardians for their young grandson, who was my age. I don't remember much about this boy because he moved away within months of arriving. The one thing I do remember is that he had more toys than anyone I had ever met. His most prized possession was a replica M-1 rifle. Given that my parents didn't much believe in guns, make-believe or real, I always had to borrow a gun from a friend if I was going to participate in our version of war games.

One day I convinced this boy to let me use the M-1 rifle that was the object of my envy. He agreed. While climbing a fence later that morning, I dropped it, and it shattered on the ground. I was heartsick. But I wasn't nearly as upset as my friend, who demanded immediate reparations. Upset and fearful, I had to tell my mother what had happened. I'm not sure which was worse—breaking the gun or having to deal with my disapproving parents. As best as I can remember, her reaction was far milder than I had anticipated, and within a day, the incident was behind me.

Looking back . . . Whom did you envy as a child? What did they have that you coveted? How did this affect your behavior? Were there any negative repercussions for you? Do you recall how these situations resolved themselves?

Were you jealous of anyone? Did you want the attention they were getting? What did you do to get attention? Did you succeed, or did your efforts backfire? Were you ever able to tell anyone about how you felt? What do you think these feelings said about how you felt about yourself? In what ways are you still stuck in your feelings of jealousy and envy?

Resentment

In many ways, resentment is a far more potent and dangerous emotion than anger. It's a quiet, seething form of anger that can burrow into your soul and make you physically, emotionally, and spiritually sick. Resentment can also drive a deep wedge between you and the others you once loved or cared for. More insidiously, it can keep you stuck and prevent you from facing the present and moving on with your life.

I have seen firsthand how resentment has destroyed hallowed relationships. A number of years ago, a good friend's uncle bailed his father out of a bad investment. Through this time, they continued speculatively to buy properties together. When they decided to sell off a parcel that had appreciated little through the years, their agreement for splitting the profits became a point of contention. After my friend's dad agreed to arbitration to settle the matter, his uncle was dissatisfied with how the arbitration was handled and ended up suing my friend's father.

My friend was horrified and indignant on hearing this. Certain that his uncle was in the wrong, he called him. What he heard was a very different story than that told by his father. For years, his uncle's resentment had been building. From his perspective, he had kept my friend's father floating through difficult times. To add insult to injury, he had put up the money for the contested deal and was making less than if he had invested in a low-yield savings account ten years earlier. He was angry and felt no appreciation coming from my friend's father for what he had done. Perhaps these resentments had their roots in their childhoods. In all probability, no one will ever know. It was clear that my friend's uncle was taking a stand, and also that he'd had enough.

Subsequently, they have spent hundreds of thousands of dollars suing and countersuing each other. Each was right, and both were wrong.

Looking back . . . What are the things or people that you have deeply resented in your life? Did you ever resent a sibling as you were growing up? How did you deal with your resentment? Did you quietly suffer with it, or did you take a stand, like my friend's uncle? How did your resentment hurt you? How did it hurt others?

Whom do you resent today? What's the price you're paying for harboring these feelings? Do any of your resentments have roots in your childhood? How did they begin?

Fear

It's impossible to live without fear, but it can also be the most crippling of all the emotions. As a child, the simplest of things can become like monsters, feeding on our imagination's ability to transform shadows into dread.

When I was young, my father would come home after work and turn on the sprinklers. They were run by a pump in a small shed at the back of our property. Around nine each night, he'd ask me to turn off the water. There was nothing I hated or feared more than this. First, I turned on the floodlights that illuminated our side and back yards. Slowly walking toward the pump house, I mustered my courage and entered into the dark, cobweb-infested structure. At first, I couldn't see anything. In the far corner was the switch. Like a blind man, I'd feel my way around the many tools stacked up there, hoping that nothing would bite me or land on my arm. *Click*. The switch was thrown, and I'd run out of there as fast as I could. Then I had to go around to the back of the building and turn off the valve. It must have taken ten turns before I heard the water hiss and stop flowing. Every shadow scared me. Sounds of the night made me tremble. Running as fast as my legs would carry me, I sprinted to my back door. My parents could never understand why I was out of breath every time I returned.

Looking back . . . What were your worst fears when you were growing up? Were there things in your room that scared you? In your closet? Under your bed? Did you face your fears alone, or did you call your parents for help? Do you recall a time when you stopped fearing certain things? What new fears replaced these old ones? Which of your childhood fears do you still have?

Sadness and Grief

As a culture, these are the emotions we collectively avoid the most. Sadness and grief are an embarrassment in this society, and an impediment to the wheels of commerce. They're something to be gotten over quickly and decisively. But childhood hurts and losses don't follow such rules.

When I was eight, I went off to camp and fell in love with the loveliest girl I had ever met. I think I wanted to marry her. The conclusion of camp was the saddest day of my life. Never again did I see her or hear from her. And there was no one in my family who truly understood the depth of my pain. I quietly persevered and suffered, like so many of us today who silently mourn our losses.

Looking back . . . What were the saddest times in your child-hood? What happened? What kinds of losses did you suffer in these early years? What kinds of consolation did you receive? Was it okay to cry? Or, did you hold it in and cry only in private?

Were there other people in your life who were also sad? How did this affect you? What did you do to console them?

What sadness do you still carry from your childhood? To this day, which old memories bring up tears? What's the one loss from childhood you still haven't fully grieved over?

Greed

Greed is a complicated emotion that can destroy relationships and lives. When we are children, greed can express itself in a benign lusting after toys and other material objects. But in adults, greediness is an ugly thing that is socially condemned.

It's hard to take a candid look at how greed operates in our own lives. For me, I find it emerging when I feel insecure and vulnerable. Suddenly, I'm in a fantasy of ten years from now, my wife has died, and I'm wondering if there's going to be enough in the insurance policy to sustain me. Such a fantasy belies my own resourcefulness. If allowed more space in my current life, it could drive a wedge between Elizabeth and me. Without consciousness, greed can overrun our lives.

Looking back . . . How were you greedy as a child? What were your prized possessions that you wouldn't share with anyone? Under what conditions would you generously let someone else play with or handle these things? Were you ever punished for being greedy or stingy? How did your greed affect your popularity with other kids your age? In what ways are you still greedy today?

Shame

Shame and guilt bind and incapacitate us. If we are taught to be shameful, we may have to spend the rest of our lives unraveling the confining tentacles that keep us from embracing our deepest selves. But we may have good reasons to be ashamed of many things we did in our childhoods.

Nearly twenty-five years ago, I was meditating. From a quiet place, the image of a dead bird filled my awareness. It was a dove that I had shot with a friend's pellet gun when I was nine years old. We weren't hunting for food. The simple thrill of killing an animal was all that we were seeking. Fifteen years after the event I found myself sitting in my bedroom overcome with remorse and guilt. Through my tears I asked that dove to forgive me for being so callous and cavalier about its precious life.

Looking back . . . As you reflect upon your childhood, what things did you feel ashamed about? Which of these were discovered by an adult, and which ones did you hide? To what lengths did you go to hide your shame? How did it feel if you confessed your guilt or were discovered? Was there a sense of relief? What things were so shameful that you couldn't tell anyone about them? What happened to make you feel this way? How do you still feel ashamed of these things as an adult?

Joy

I had so many joys as a child. Running, playing, riding my bike, swimming, skiing, tennis, golf, and even learning. There were times when I'd laugh so hard that I thought I'd die. And there were special times with my dad, like when we caught what seemed like every trout in Tampa Bay.

Looking back . . . What were the things that made you happy as a child? What were your favorite pastimes? Sports? Games? Imaginary journeys and adventures? Whom did you like spending time with in your family? What are your fondest memories of that person? Were there any special times of the day that made you the happiest? When did you feel the most freedom? Can you ever remember a time when you were so excited about an upcoming event that you couldn't sleep? What were your passions at that time? What things could you do for hours and not tire of? What gave you the greatest satisfaction? What was the happiest day of your childhood?

Kindness

The best of who we are shines through our acts of kindness. I have witnessed children acting with a gentle and kind touch that seems to have preceded socialization. As small-minded as children can be, they can also generously include others who have been ostracized, and stand up for those who are incapable of standing up for themselves.

Looking back . . . Think back on your life in seven-year increments. When do you recall feeling kindness toward another person? Can you recall any acts of your kindness or generosity when you were young? How did you help a friend or a sibling? What things were you willing to share? Did you ever lend money to someone not knowing whether or not they could repay you? Did you ever go out of your way to lend a hand?

Other Emotions

There are hundreds of nuances to the emotions listed above. You can explore each in the manner previously discussed. Here's a list that may spur your thinking and recollection:

abandoned	foolish	passionate
annoyed	fulfilled	selfish
anxious	funny	sentimental
blue	hostile	sexy
confident	humiliated	shy
cunning	hurt	silly
defeated	inhibited	strong
defensive	intimidated	tense
depressed	lonely	tired
disappointed	longing	vibrant
ecstatic	lust	vulnerable
embarrassed	macho	weak
enthusiastic	overloaded	worried

All of the memory work we have done to this point has prepared the foundation for the deeper learning and healing that personal stories can provide. In the coming chapters, I will introduce you to a variety of methods that can help you transform the pain of these stories into sacred and cherished narratives.

CHAPTER 13

The Learning Way

In *Speaking in Stories* by William White, he recounts a conversation between a master and his disciple that captures the heart of the learning way.

> A disciple once complained, "You tell us stories, but you never reveal their meaning to us."
>
> Said the master, "How would you like it if someone offered you fruit and chewed it up before giving it to you?"
>
> No one can find your meaning for you.
> Not even the master.

Until now, we have been exploring tools for recovering the past. In itself, this is a worthy enterprise, and if you were to stop here and do no more than share your life stories with family and friends, you would be handsomely rewarded. But story can also be a powerful vehicle for uncovering new meanings, learning, and wisdom. Herein lies the real value of this journey.

In this chapter, you'll learn about ancient and contemporary approaches to viewing your stories, and how you can make them relevant to your present concerns. I'll also show you how to unlock lessons that can nourish your soul and lead you onto the path of healing.

A Native American Model for Listening and Learning

Nearly two hundred years ago there was an Oneida community living on the Shenango River in western Pennsylvania. Almost since the arrival of the first Europeans on the shores of New England, Native Americans were forced to adapt and change in response to the pressures of an expanding population of settlers. In the process, many of the old and cherished traditions and rituals were lost or cast aside.

It was in this context that Paula Underwood's great-great-grandmother received an important teaching that was transmitted across five generations to Paula. Paula's great-great-grandmother was young, perhaps no more than sixteen or seventeen, and an apprentice healer in her community. One of her first patients was an old man who was clearly dying. He had been the "Keeper of the Old Ways." To the young people, these things seemed irrelevant to their present concerns and the Oneida's current circumstances. Few were interested in hearing, much less learning, this knowledge.

It was not clear why this man was dying. Paula's great-great-grandmother's task was to discover the cause and cure him. She discovered that what ailed him was grief. No one was willing to learn all that he had to share. He knew that with his death all of the knowledge acquired by his ancestors would die with him.

The young woman was moved by this and agreed to learn all of the ancient stories and old ways. This was a daunting task. The stories he knew spanned ten thousand years. To learn, know, and understand the meaning of each required an enormous commitment. In spite of this, and the uncertainty that faced her and her tribe, she accepted the responsibility of becoming a link to the ancestors.

Something remarkable happened each day as she carefully listened. His health slowly improved. By the time she had learned all of the ancient stories and teachings, he was healed.

Through the last two hundred years these stories have been passed down in Paula's family. When she turned three, her father began the slow process of educating her in this Native way of seeing and understanding. Prophetically, her great-great-grandmother planned that these learnings would be preserved as a gift for all peoples and that they would someday be crafted and written down by her descendants five generations later. Paula has fulfilled that wish. Her writings now include *The Walking People: A Native American Oral History; Who Speaks for Wolf: A Native American Learning Story;* and *Three Strands in the Braid: A Guide for Enablers of Learning.*

It's been my good fortune to learn and study with Paula. Many of the following ideas are drawn from my understanding of her teachings, but have been personally refocused and adapted to address the concerns of using story as a tool to heal our lives.

In this Native approach to seeing and thinking, all things are perceived as a wholeness, whereas in our culture, we splinter things apart. Native Americans, in general, would not have made a clear distinction between intuition and logic or art and mathematics. Each of these distinct modalities or disciplines is part of a continuum. When seen in this way, together they give us a depth of perception that is not available when we see the world through only one paradigm. Likewise, the components of a story—imagery and language—are two parts of the same perception, each leading to a different understanding. One without the other is impossible.

Paula's Native American tradition also understood the functioning of our brain's two hemispheres. While they didn't use language like left and right brain, they recognized that there are distinct functions that deal with spoken or written language versus pictures or images. For a story to be absorbed and understood in its completeness, each of these functions must be engaged. When we hear or tell a story, it is initially a right-brain affair. Pictures, images, feelings, and sensations are the language of this hemisphere. But in order to perceive things as a whole, they understood that we must also engage the linear and analytic functions that are associated with the left brain. This is accomplished by asking a simple, but powerful, question: "What might we learn from this?" By finishing a story with a question, we or the listener are invited to contemplate its meaning.

On the other hand, at the conclusion, fables and moral stories offer up the meaning of the story in a succinct fashion. But once you tell the person what you expect them to think or see, they become involved in a left-brain dance, growing more inclined to memorize an appropriate, logical response than to dig for a deeper answer that's personally relevant. Nonverbal, intuitive learning, which is essential to integrated thinking, is lost.

In contrast, the Native American learning story invites the listener to grapple with the story's meaning and draw his or her own conclusions. From this perspective, fables and their explicit messages short-circuit the learning process. Only when the learner is looking within herself for answers is there inter-lobal communication between the left and right hemispheres. Something remarkable happens when we ask the question, "What might I learn from this?" We are encouraged to enter into the story and see it from our own perspective, wrestling with its meaning to us at this moment in time. There are no right answers—just different ways of seeing. As such, story becomes a vehicle for self-taught learning.

This tradition holds that you cannot teach another person. There are only structures from which you can learn. In fact, there's no word for "teach" in the ancient Oneida language. From this perspective, the best we can do is *enable learning* by presenting through spoken language vivid pictures and images for the mind, thereby stimulating right-brain activity. Then, by asking an incisive question, we encourage left- and right-brain communication.

Through the years, this tradition developed a number of stories that were designed to engender questions, not answers, and to raise issues, not resolve them. By applying this same approach to personal stories, we can open up our own questioning minds to areas of deeper meaning.

For example, what might I learn from my story "Christmas on Terrace Drive"? Think along with me and ask yourself what you might learn. My first thought is that, as a young boy, I was hungry for recognition and would do nearly anything for attention. How is that true for me today? As I contemplate this idea, I'm aware that my creative pursuits are tied up with this notion of being important in others' eyes. That truth is hard for me to swallow.

What else might I learn from this story? My thoughts turn to my mother, who was a guardian of the Jewish tradition in our home. Suddenly, I respect her more for trying to maintain our own customs. I wonder how my own laxness about my beliefs has played out in my life, and what was gained and what was lost by my mother bowing to my insistence that we buy a Christmas tree.

My thoughts turn to my father and my feeling that he was barely present in my life. How am I not present today for my wife and stepson? In what ways have I assumed the same workaholic traits? How do I still hold back my affections from those I love?

By applying this approach to any story that comes from our life experiences, or one that we hear from another person, we can open ourselves to new learning. Whether a story's content is negative or positive, painful or joyful, it can be redeemed by serving the higher purpose of asking the incisive question, "What might we learn from this?"

The Medicine Wheel*

Medicine wheels have played important roles in many traditional cultures—assisting in the resolution of conflicts, deepening the spiritual journey, and facilitating the process of learning. In her work, Paula Underwood has introduced an ancestral wheel that weaves together a tapestry of meaning from the many ingredients of learning. When stories are "put on the wheel," their relevance can unfold in new and unexpected ways.

The Circumference of the Wheel

The wheel has the following components that span its circumference—sensitivity, perception, inspiration, understanding, communication, growth, community, individuality, introspection, conflict, peace, and wisdom. Each of these elements can open our life experiences to new interpretations. To use the wheel as a tool for looking at your personal stories, proceed in a clockwise direction and answer the following questions. Note that the questions move from the particular to the universal.

Sensitivity: How can this story help you become more sensitive to the physical and social world around you? In what ways was your insensitivity or the callousness of others a factor in the story? How has sensitivity played a role in your life? Do you consider yourself to be a sensitive person? How does this show up in your actions? Can you think of other stories that demonstrate this trait?

*Copyright ©1995, Paula Underwood. The Medicine Wheel is reproduced here by permission of Paula Underwood. Paula presents the Medicine Wheel, the Great Hoop of Life, in a very different manner than the application presented in this text. In addition to teaching the Wheel as part of the "Past Is Prologue Educational Program" (approved by the U.S. Department of Education as an Exemplary Education Program), she is also presently preparing a book to share this wisdom.

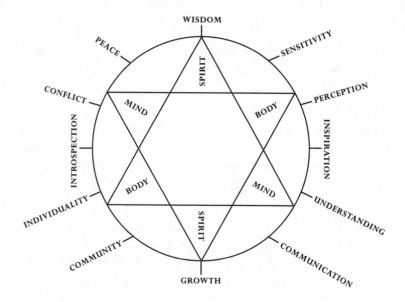

Perception: How does this story expand the scope of your perception? Which of the five senses come into play? Do certain senses dominate your stories? What is your favorite sense? Least favorite? What might you learn from this?

Inspiration: How does inspiration play a role in this story? How can your story help you open up to and use your inspiration to assist you when you're confronted with problems? Can you think of other stories in which inspiration, or the lack of it, played a role? If you cannot find stories in which inspiration played a factor in the resolution of difficult situations, what do you make of that? Is it missing altogether in your life? How can you find it?

Understanding: How does this story deepen and broaden your understanding of yourself and others? To what degree did misunderstanding play a role in the story? Are you an understanding person? When do you have little patience for understanding?

Communication: To what degree is this a story about communication? How did miscommunication affect the story's outcome? What can you learn from this story about the manner in which you communicated then and now? How were things communicated in your household?

Growth: How does this story reflect your personal growth and the growth of others? Does this story display your failure to grow and change? How can you grow from the lessons contained in the story? How do you view personal growth? How do you know that you have grown?

Community: What constituted your community at the time of this story? To what degree is this a story about others versus about you? How were decisions made in this story? Through consensus or autocratically? How important was community to you then? Now? How are you still connected to this original community?

Individuality: To what degree is this a story about preserving your individuality and autonomy while being a part of a group? Were you successful in your struggle? How can you learn from this struggle when you look at your life today? Do you consider yourself an individualist or a joiner? Has that always been true of you?

Introspection: To what degree did solitude play a role in this particular story? In your childhood? Did you like being alone? How did you pass the time? How did you grapple with feelings of loneliness? Is it comfortable to look inside and inspect your feelings and thoughts? Where is the discomfort?

Conflict: Were there conflicts in this story? How were they re-solved? Were you the instigator of the conflict? How has con-flict affected your life? Were you comfortable with conflict as a child? Was it handled constructively? What kinds of hurts do you have over the conflicts of your life?

Peace: Is this a story about peace? Can you derive a sense of peace from the story as you tell it now? To what degree was your child-hood peaceful and filled with harmonious feelings? How was peace maintained in your household? Who was the peacemaker?

Wisdom: How can you integrate your answers to all of the above questions into a cohesive whole? What pieces are still missing? Where did you learn wisdom as a child? Did you have a men-tor as you were growing up? How did your bad judgment be-come a source of learning and wisdom?

The Inner Triangle

Last, as you can see in the diagram of the Medicine Wheel, there is a triangle in the center, with body, mind, and spirit at each apex. In our culture, we have made clear distinctions between these three elements of life, but in this model they are the un-derpinnings for all human activity. Moreover, they are part of a continuum that is not burdened with hierarchies. Each provides a perspective through which to see life events and experiences.

Body: As you tell or hear the story, what is your bodily reaction? How does it feel in your gut? If you were hurt physically, where was the wound? Were you grounded at the time of this story, or totally in your head?

Mind: From the viewpoint of the mind, how were you thinking at the time of this story? What were your mental preoccupa-tions? Were you mindful of the world around you? How did you use your intellect to solve life problems? Did you have street smarts?

Spirit: What are the spiritual implications of this tale? How did these events deepen your spirituality, if at all? How did they violate your spirit? Were you living from this center, or were you more involved with mental and bodily activity? Were there any other players in the story whose behavior and demeanor exhibited this spiritual connection?

The Rule of Six

So often we rush to judgment when it comes to our stories. Meaning can easily be wrapped into a neat package that superficially satisfies our need for closure. These kinds of conclusions are all too familiar. "He was an abusive father." "I come from a dysfunctional family." "She's so obsessive." "He can't be trusted." When *this* exclusively means *that,* and *that* only means *this*, we close the book on learning and there is no further opportunity for growth or understanding. The deeper possibilities of the story are lost.

By pursuing alternative meanings to your stories you can set yourself free. Paula Underwood has introduced another incisive tool that can facilitate this process of story exploration—the Rule of Six. Originally, her Native American tradition developed the Rule of Six to improve decision making. It was understood that solutions that were given little credence often turned out to be the best decisions, and that the obvious and commonsense options were frequently misleading. They needed a way to encourage people to dig for their answers and look at all the possibilities. Interestingly, the Rule of Six can be applied differently for each side of the brain.

In *Three Strands in the Braid*, Paula explains how it works for the right side of the brain. Our world is so complex that no one thing can be the cause for another. Most of us, though, are stuck in a Newtonian, linear model of personal reality—"a" strikes "b," causing "c" to move. In contrast, the Rule of Six says, "For every perceivable phenomenon, devise at least six plausible explanations that indeed explain the phenomenon. There are probably sixty, but if you devise six, this will sensitize you to the complexity of the universe, the variability of perception. It will prevent you from fixing on the first plausible explanation as The Truth."

As an example, we could apply the Rule of Six to "Christmas on Terrace Drive" by asking, "Why did my father rarely give me the attention and affection that I needed?" Here are six possible explanations, each of which holds some truth in my mind: 1) my dad was working so hard that he didn't have time; 2) he was uncomfortable expressing affection and love; 3) his father never gave him this kind of affection, so he never learned how to give it; 4) once boys reach a certain age in our culture, there is a taboo against fathers touching their sons; 5) he believed that it was my mother's role to offer this kind of encouragement; and 6) my dad was very unhappy at this time and was depressed about the kind of work he was having to do. He simply didn't have the emotional resources to give me very much.

Through this kind of perspective, the story not only opens itself up to new interpretations, but I am opened up to seeing my father with less judgment and more compassion. Each of these explanations has implications for the past as well as my present. If my dad didn't learn how to give affection from his dad, and I didn't learn it from him, must I unconsciously participate in this legacy? I think not. There are many avenues available for developing this side of myself. I am now empowered to write a new script that can change future generations.

When looked at from the left side of the brain, where the more analytic and linear thought processes reside, we now assign a probability factor to each of the above explanations. This is highly subjective. Your appraisal may differ radically from mine. None of the probabilities can be 100 percent, and never can we assign a 0 percent probability. By following this procedure, everything in the world of our stories becomes tentative, never fixed. Even the ideas we assign to a 95 percent probability are open to reexamination. In the above example, I assign 90 percent probabilities to numbers 1 and 3. To number 6 I assign a 70 percent probability, and so on. Regardless of the percentage allotted to each, I now have a tool for expanding my understanding of my personal reality. This not only sheds light on the dynamic forces that shaped my childhood, it also illuminates who I am today.

Divining Assumptions

Encapsulated in every perspective and belief is a core assumption. For example, a few months before my mother died, she called, begging me to finish my doctorate degree in psychology even though I had built up a very successful company. She even offered to pay for it. When I suggested that what I really wanted was to go back to school to get an M.F.A. in painting, she immediately withdrew her support. I didn't expect her to go along with my suggestion, and, at the time, I found it humorous. I suspect, though, that one of her core assumptions was that for me to be *somebody* in the world, I had to have an advanced degree. Given her overidentification with her kids, it may be that for *her* to be somebody, I needed that degree.

Every story we tell about our self or another person carries the seeds of assumption that affect why the story is told, how it's told, and what it means to us. And each character in the story acted out of some assumption. In the Christmas story about my father, he no doubt presupposed that as a child I was getting everything I needed. If he had known this was untrue, I have no doubt that he would have acted differently.

By asking ourselves what limiting assumptions were operating at the time a story took place, we peel away a layer of reality to discover a deeper truth. It's most likely that we'll find a common thread that weaves together many of our stories. Once this particular assumption is brought to light, we can reexamine the facts of these stories with an eye toward a different conclusion. For example, if you had learned to be a victim early in life, no doubt many of your stories would lend credence to the fact that everyone was out to get you. But, if you can examine your stories with a conscious eye and see this assumption, the stories will change. They will no longer be about what other people did to you, but rather about what you did to invite other people to hurt and abuse you. The fact of your being wounded will not change, but everything else will.

Freeing Assumptions

If we are willing to look at our stories as tools for transformation, they can lead us to a new relationship with our self and open us to new beliefs and freer patterns of behavior. For example, many of the stories I have told about my father revolve around the theme that he simply wasn't available to me when I was growing up. Then, I didn't feel important or loved. It's not surprising that I carried many of these feelings into my adult life. They no longer serve me, but I often feel stuck with them. There can be a shift, though, by asking an incisive question that is adapted from the work of Nancy Kline in her book *Women and Power: How Far Can We Go?*: If you knew that [*a phrase that embodies a new assumption that replaces the limiting assumption that kept us stuck as a child, and now as an adult*], how would that make you feel now?

Here's how I would adapt it to the scenario I described above. "If I knew that *my father loved me as a child, and that I was important to him*, how would that make me feel now?" By being willing to step into a space predicated on a new, freeing assumption, I open up my emotional landscape. If I knew that he felt that way toward me, it would make me now feel that everything in my world is all right. In a strange way, I sense my insides to be more spacious. I experience in this moment the joy that love brings me. The facts of the past recede and what emerges is the present, imagined reality. Remember, the body does not know the difference between a real event and an imagined one. When we imagine what it would feel like if something good happened, even if it didn't, we get to taste, perhaps for the first time, what we longed for all of our lives.

Now retell your stories with this new feeling in mind. What shows up for you as you reinterpret the past from this new stance of wholeness? For me, what appears is a story filled with forgiveness and understanding. Instead of choosing to emphasize how my father never came to any of my Little League games, I can talk about how hard he worked to see that I had everything I needed in order to participate. I can even talk about my love for baseball without it being overlaid by statements such as that my dad never saw me play, or rarely had time to toss the ball with me. It hurt that he couldn't come, but it wasn't because he didn't love me. Now, I no longer need him to come to the games. In my mind, I have brought him there. I have savored the experience, and it has filled me with what I desired most as a child.

While storytelling can be an enriching and entertaining journey, its real fruits are experienced when we apply the eyes of learning to every facet of the past. From learning we receive strength, distance, understanding, compassion, and, most of all, healing. Now that you are equipped with the rudimentary learning tools, let's proceed to the next chapter to deepen our healing journey.

CHAPTER 14

The Healing Path

You will not grow if you sit in a beautiful garden and somebody brings you gorgeous food on a silver platter. But you will grow if you are sick, if you are in pain, if you experience losses, and if you do not put your head in the sand, but take the pain and learn to accept it, not as a curse or a punishment, but as a gift to you with a very, very specific purpose.

—Elisabeth Kübler-Ross, "Death Does Not Exist"

Seeing our deepest hurts and wounds as gifts is easier said than done. At first blush, Kübler-Ross's words may even sound like New Age idealism. I know that my first reaction to a painful experience or troublesome period in my life is to wish that it hadn't happened, that it would go away, and that somehow I could excise it from my being. If only I were a different person who had grown up in better circumstances! Ironically, the more I have rejected or denied my pains, the more dominant they have become in my life. They don't go away. Instead, they go underground, only to reemerge as chronic emotional and physical ailments. Unfortunately, in this altered state they are rarely identifiable.

To stand face to face with our pains and wounds requires great courage and a deep willingness to forgive. It also demands of us that we open ourselves up to being changed in unpredictable ways by the re-storying of our lives. Through the suggestions that follow I cannot promise you that every painful and difficult experience will be transformed into a jewel, and that each wound of the past will be totally healed. The pain may persist, but it will no longer be meaningless. The scars will still be visible, but I hope that you will discover learning and purpose as you explore their jagged edges. In this way, story can become a healing, redeeming force in your life.

Transforming the Wound

Ironically, it's how we tell our stories of past woundings that frequently keeps us stuck. The wound itself is not the culprit.

Remember my earlier example of how my practical joke with the fake ink spill backfired? The conclusion to this story is still unclear in my mind. I vaguely recall the doorbell ringing. It was one of my mom's friends. My mother ushered me into the pantry and told me to change clothes and stop crying. Alone and frightened, I put on new clothes and slipped down the hallway to my room. Nothing was ever said about the incident, but our relationship was never quite the same after that.

There are several ways to work with stories like this. Obviously, it's highly charged. I recall telling this tale in a counseling session years ago. Even though I was pained, I couldn't really get to the heart of the emotion. Using a different technique, I revisited this story three years ago and was able to find completion. Here's how.

Shifting Tenses

Every story has many levels. Originally, I recounted this story as though it were about someone else, describing it as an event in the distant past while also belittling its significance. It was difficult for me to identify with the little battered boy in the story. In contrast, entering the story as though it were occurring right now helped me to access the deep hurt I have stored. This can be accomplished by retelling the story in the present tense.

If you carry a painful story like this one, find a committed listener who will hold the space for this kind of exploration. Retell your story in the present tense, as if it were happening to you in this very moment. More important, stay close to the physicality of the story. Describe in present terms each thing that happened. If you are the listener, bring the teller back to each element of the story, requesting explicit descriptions in place of global statements. At each pivotal point, ask how it feels and where it hurts.

In my example, I would tell you something like, "My mother sees me giggling. Suddenly, out of nowhere, she hits me across the head. I'm frightened! She hits me again. I'm trying to cover up, but it doesn't help. She hits me across the left ear. The entire side of my face stings. . . ." As I told this story in this way, allowing myself to be the seven-year-old, I got to the deep hurt and well of tears, and sobbed for nearly an hour. Only after going through this experience could I begin to see my mother as anything but an awful person for doing this. I even felt compassion and understanding. She must have been so ashamed of her own behavior that she didn't know how to face me. Today, I can understand that and can forgive her.

By retelling your stories in this way, I believe you, too, can find healing and forgiveness. Don't rush it. You may need to repeat the process several times until you reach the painful truth of your stories. Only then can you cease to be a victim of their consequences.

Exploring the Story's Images

Another tool for moving into the depth of the story is to apply a traditional tool from Gestalt dream analysis to each of the story's images. Begin by telling the story to another person, or, if you choose, write down the story. Then, list the many dominant images, characters, and actions in the story. In the above story about spilled ink, the following stand out for me: "little boy playing a prank," "older brother helping little boy play a prank," "the ink bottle and fake spill," "mother entering the dining room to find her new marble stained," "little boy giggling," "mother lashing out in anger," "little boy frightened," "little boy in pantry changing clothes," "mother talking with visitor," and "mother not coming to the little boy to discuss what happened."

If you are unfamiliar with Gestalt dream analysis, in its simplest form you, the dreamer, are asked to identify with each of the elements of the dream, including the inanimate ones, speaking as though you are that element. The idea is to get to how you feel as that thing, person, or action. From this perspective, all aspects of the dream are part of you.

In the same way, each facet of your personal stories is also part of you. In the above example, I would say, "I am the little boy playing a prank, and I feel. . . ." Or, "I am the spilled ink, and I feel. . . ." Or, "I am my mother, lashing out in anger, and I feel. . . ." At first, this may seem awkward, or even contrived. Don't settle for the first thing that comes to mind. Mull over each phrase. Seriously consider the story from the viewpoint of that person or thing. Even though the ink is inanimate, its role in this story is central. When given a voice, it may express what none of the characters could speak.

What you will find is that this process opens you up to hidden dimensions of the story that are not apparent when everything is seen from the perspective of you, the protagonist. If you were the victim in your story, seeing the action from the victimizer's vantage point may seem unthinkable at first. Be willing to play with the process. Try it on knowing that as much as you may detest this person, you may discover that there are parts of this person that are redeemable. There are also parts of yourself that you have neatly contained that may be filled with similar violence, hate, and rage. By being willing to see this story as that person saw it, you can also redeem all the aspects of your own personality that have been difficult to accept and integrate.

Finding Forgiveness

In *The Spirituality of Imperfection*, Kurtz and Ketcham describe the terrible price we can pay for not forgiving. In this brief exchange, we can see that a hardened heart ultimately victimizes no one but ourselves.

> A former inmate of a Nazi concentration camp was visiting a friend who had shared the ordeal with him.
> "Have you forgiven the Nazis?" he asked his friend.
> "Yes."
> "Well, I haven't. I'm still consumed with hatred for them."
> "In that case," said his friend gently, "they still have you in prison."

Resentment, grudges, unexpressed anger, and past injustices can all imprison us. Unfortunately, the people whom we hold responsible for these unfinished feelings usually don't suffer because of our feelings. We're the ones who continue to pay the price by keeping alive the story in its current form. In a sense, we perpetuate the victimization, only now it's our own stories that inflict the wound. Instead of being the author of our stories, we're bit players with no power to change the script or even suggest a different conclusion. Forgiveness is hard to come by when we are mired in such powerful scripts, because these stories don't exist for us as imagined realities, but look as real as any three-dimensional object. How can we move out of this conundrum?

The first step is to reframe the nature of the story, the victimizer's intent, and the consequences of his or her actions.

Begin by making a list of all the people who have wronged you in your life. One by one, consider your story about what happened, how you were hurt by this person's actions, and the effect he or she has had on your life. How do you feel about this person?

Now emotionally step away from the story and ask yourself, "What did I learn from this experience with this person?" You may have to dig deep. Try to frame your response in positive terms. For example, if you were Eve in the Garden of Eden, you might find it difficult to forgive the serpent for leading you to your downfall. You may have been replaying over and over again the fateful decision to trust his advice. If you pause from this incessant cacophony of recrimination and blame, you may find redeeming aspects to the experience. For example, you might have learned that all things are not as they appear; that through the knowledge of good and evil you now have a sense of freedom that was absent in your earlier consciousness; that trust is a fragile thing; and that it helps to have a history with a person before we entrust him or her with things as important as our future.

Once you have recognized the lessons you gleaned from this painful injustice, verbally thank the person who wronged you for the opportunity to learn and grow. Acknowledge how difficult the experience was and how much, at the time, it hurt you. Also, affirm that the persons who wronged you were either ignorant of their actions or had to have been coming from a very painful place themselves. If you know what affected their actions, let them know in your internal, private dialogue that you now understand the difficulties that, at the time, affected their behavior. If you do not know, imagine at this time what may have occurred to make them act the way they did. Search for reasons that imply that they also violated their better natures and acted out of fear or hurt themselves.

There's a well-used phrase in the world of twelve-step programs—fake it until you make it. In many ways, we may have to fake forgiveness by imagining reasons to justify our lenity before we can really feel it and believe it.

Becoming Our Own Author

To transform your pain, you must become the author of your own story. Assuming authorship gives you complete literary license to do whatever you choose. It's your life and your story. As author, you are father and mother to yourself. Stories that enslave you in the here and now can be recrafted to empower a different outcome. And, like a nurturing parent, you can gently select new aspects of your story to emphasize, freeing you to experience new feelings and possibilities.

A powerful way to transform your tales is to play with their modality. We now know that humor is a physical and emotional healing force. When we can laugh at ourselves and the facts of our life, it will not change what happened, but we will be changed and released from the heavy burden of tragedy and misfortune. Even the most sacrosanct subjects are open to this form of review. For example, when my mother suffered a stroke in 1983, my brother and I assumed the responsibility for arranging the funeral. She had been deteriorating over the last twenty-four hours, and the doctors had told us that once her respirator was detached, she would live for only a few minutes. In the midst of this sad drama, we went to the funeral home to select a casket. Given that Jewish law dictates a wooden casket, our choices were narrowed. The director guided us upstairs, where a sample of each model was handsomely displayed. Until we asked, he didn't mention a thing about price. His sales presentation focused strictly on the fine workmanship of each casket. My brother interrupted him. "What's the difference between these two? You say this one is six hundred dollars more, but they look exactly the same." With a straight face the director informed us that the difference was like night and day. While the first casket was a quality product (they would not be offering it otherwise!), the more expensive model could command such a high price because it used dowels made of oak instead of metal. My brother and I looked at each other. We looked at the casket. Then we looked at the somber face of our casket salesman and broke into hysterical laughter.

I think my mother would have appreciated this ludicrous scene. She had a great sense of humor and would have been laughing, too. When I tell about her passing, I choose to focus on this story rather than the unpleasant details of the hospital and the enormous grief we all experienced. Even in dying she made us laugh, and that's the way I'd like to remember her.

Another way to rewrite horrific stories is to retell them comedically. In a workshop a few years ago, a woman told of a time when she was being transported to the hospital in an ambulance after a nasty accident. None of her injuries was life threatening, but she was badly bruised and hurting. When the ambulance pulled to a stop and the attendant and driver told her they'd be right back, she was perplexed and curious. Propping herself up so that she could see through the windshield, she was shocked. They were at an Arby's, and the two paramedics were stopping for a bite to eat. At the time, this was a scene out of *The Twilight Zone.* But in the retelling, this woman turned this crazy scene into high comedy. Everyone at her table could hardly stay in their seats from the laughter.

Take some of the most difficult moments of your life and retell them as though they are a comedy. Notice how you felt about these events before telling the story, and the degree to which they have a grip on your vitality, self-image, and interpersonal relationships. How do you feel now that you have brought humor to bear on the same details? What have you learned about yourself and the people involved? How does humor free you?

Re-storying Your Life

Each of us lives within the boundaries of stories that define our personality, our vocational limits, the meaning of joy and sadness, the range of our ability to form and sustain significant relationships, the definition of success and failure, ethical and moral standards, our view of life and death, and much more. These dominant stories are important because of what they have helped us to become. They are equally significant because of the ways in which they have limited and constrained our life choices and possibilities. Unfortunately, these stories are so powerful that they masquerade as deeply held beliefs, ultimate truth, and even reality.

For example, an important theme in my life is that I have never felt like I quite belong. At times it has felt more like a reality than a belief. I could find evidence in numerous places that justified this view. Now that I have examined this area in greater depth, it's easy for me to see where this belief comes from. As I was growing up, my mother frequently shared stories of how she was excluded from participating in high school clubs because she was Jewish. The local country club was not for us, because, once again, Jews were not allowed. And, my parents had many friends who were much wealthier than we were, so there were numerous activities we missed out on because we couldn't afford them. With time, I acquired my own stories of exclusion. I went to a Baptist camp two summers in a row and hid the fact that I was Jewish. This was followed by a variety of ecumenical religious experiences where being Jewish was decidedly not cool. I didn't join the Boy Scouts, because I decided it was stupid. The truth was that I had grown afraid of being part of an organization that potentially wouldn't want me as a member. Unfortunately, with time I began to live as though the outcome of these stories was a foregone conclusion—it was safer not to participate rather than risk humiliation and rejection. At this point in my life I am unhappy with the consequences of these stories. I want to participate and feel at home with others.

To shift out of this mode is not easy. First, I must seek out stories that contradict this dominant theme of isolation and loneliness. A good starting place is to focus on those experiences in which I was an active participant. For example, I played team sports throughout my adolescence. I have frequently worked on teams with other people during my professional career, and have been accepted and liked. Recalling stories of how I successfully engaged with others can put me in touch with the positive and rewarding feelings associated with these experiences. These stories are hidden resources for me. When I hesitate about joining a club or organization, I can choose to recall the times when belonging was a positive event in my life rather than dwelling on negative stories in this genre.

Likewise, if our dominant story emphasizes problems in our life, we can become a slave to these problems rather than living within a story of solutions and success. For example, we have all been so stuck that we were quick to tell others our hard-luck stories. Unfortunately, repeatedly telling these tales becomes a self-fulfilling act. If this is an issue for you, or someone you know, one sure contradiction is to retell these stories, looking for the hidden successes and lessons. Nothing is ever black and white. It's only our stories that make it so.

One form of such stories blames parents and family for all of the troubles in one's life. I know because I have been there. For years I lamented my father's unavailability, my mother's neurotic overprotection, their materialistic values, et cetera. As long as I held my family responsible for my lack of satisfaction in life, I was unable to move forward in deciding how I wanted to be. In *Care of the Soul*, Thomas Moore suggests that we shift our emphasis away from psychological analysis and blame to actually seeing the family as a source of empowering stories:

When we tell stories about the family without judgment and without instant analysis, the literal persons turn into characters in a drama and isolated episodes reveal themselves as themes in a great saga. Family history is transformed into myth. Whether we know it or not, our ideas about the family are rooted in the ways we imagine the family. . . . To care for the soul of the family, it is necessary to shift from causal thinking to an appreciation for story and character. . . . If we were to observe the soul in the family by honoring its stories and by not running away from its shadows, then we might not feel so inescapably determined by family influences. Strongly influenced by developmental psychology, we assume we are ineluctably who we are because of the family in which we grew up. What if we thought of the family less as the determining influence by which we are formed and more the raw material from which we can make a life.

As we have discussed throughout this book, the family as such is not a literal reality. Our stories about these people and their impact on our lives are the products of interpretation and imagination. They are not immutable. Rather, they can be reinterpreted at any time.

Family myths can also powerfully affect our relationships. For example, when my grandfather committed suicide, I assumed that the heart-attack story had been fabricated to protect us children from the awkwardness of the subject, and to help our parents deal with their own distress. At the time I learned of his suicide, I didn't know how to discuss this with my father, but I had a burning need to know what he knew. It took me nearly ten years to muster the courage to speak with him. I anticipated that it would be an unsettling discussion that my dad would want to avoid. When I did bring it up, all of my fears dissipated. He didn't even recall the story we had been told and was more than willing to discuss what he knew of the circumstances that surrounded his father's suicide. In that moment, I felt a tremendous weight lift. One of the most powerful taboos in my family had been broken, and I felt that I at last could begin discovering who my grandfather really was.

When seen in this way, we can begin to unravel the stories that have kept us immobilized and look for the strengths and positive qualities we learned from our family, regardless of how dysfunctional it was, rather than looking at our family legacy as a neurotic sentence that we must live with until our dying days. This means seeking alternate versions of our family stories that will open the door to personal change and transformation.

Revising Personal and Family Myths

What is your dominant story? What stories within your family have helped to reinforce these themes? How have these stories helped you? How do they keep you stuck? If you knew you had complete control over revising these stories, how would you tell them now? What alternate explanations can you find for the same set of facts? What new information do you need to help you reexamine your stories? Who can you seek out to fill in the picture? Once you have revised your story, how does it make you feel? Is the ending satisfying? Even if it's not happy, does it give you a sense of completion? Does it do justice to you and the other players in the story? How does this new picture affect the way in which you see others? If you knew that your story was valid, how would this affect the way you would act today?

As you develop new story lines, you will discover in the first telling or writing that they may seem hollow and empty. They won't carry the same weight as the time-honored tales that you've been telling yourself for years. Play with these new viewpoints. Rehearse them by telling a committed listener the same tale over and over. See what happens as you tell the tale for the third and fourth times. Notice how your sense of the story and yourself changes with each telling.

When Things Are Missing

Relatively little of our lives is ever storied. Most of our experiences and perceptions flow into the amorphous black hole that we call our past, never to be recalled, reflected on, or evaluated. A major focus of this book is to assist you in the sometimes arduous task of reconstructing and reflecting on these memories. But do not be surprised if you discover that there are some areas of your childhood where there seem to be no stories at all. As hard as you try, you may be unable to retrieve any information about a specific place or time. This is not uncommon, and is not a sign of impending senility. Rather, these disruptions in the continuity of your stories can be in itself an important feature of your story that is worthy of exploration.

The first step is to notice these lapses and view them with detached interest. What kinds of significant events occurred at that time or in that place? Did you suffer through a difficult trauma, such as the death of a parent? Were you the victim of some sort of emotional or physical abuse? Were you continually uprooted, moving more than once a year? Was it a happy time or a period filled with sadness? Do you know why? What was happening between your parents? Were they having marital difficulties? Did you spend a lot of time alone, or were you involved with your parents and other kids your age?

As we discussed earlier, when traumatic events occur in our lives, they demand to be storied if the healing is to begin. If these experiences go unstoried, for whatever reason, they often become occluded and inaccessible.

There are many ways in which you can work with this issue. My first advice is to go slowly. These things often unravel with time. A few years ago, a good friend of mine claimed that he couldn't remember anything in his childhood before the age of ten or eleven. I was astonished, but he meant it. He could barely describe the inside of his house. After further discussion I learned that he didn't even have his own bedroom—he slept on a pull-out bed in the dining room. The emotional climate was explosive. With no place he could call his own, and living in what was tacitly a combat zone, it was understandable that the process of storying his life was disrupted. Over the last few years, though, as he has willingly explored his emotional life, more and more details have surfaced. Even positive experiences have emerged from this period.

There are other times when we have little or no knowledge of a significant period of our lives because we lived in a sterile environment in which parents shared little or nothing from their pasts. A friend's father died when he was sixteen. His mother died only a few years later. There were entire wings of his house that he had hardly set foot in because they were only for adults. He rarely saw his father, and was thrust into the role of parenting his mother after his dad's tragic and sudden death. Only recently was he able to begin constructing parts of his childhood by visiting his mom's hometown, where an elderly cousin still lives. By hearing stories of his mother's childhood and her courageous step to leave a small Southern town and venture to a large city in the Northeast, he was able to begin piecing together aspects of his childhood that had always been baffling. Many of the details, though, will never be recovered. Under such circumstances, there is a third option available that I have used to re-create family stories.

The Role of Archaeologist

A family myth I repeatedly heard during my childhood was that my mother's father, George, stole his brother's ticket to come to America. Another piece of the story that was even more intriguing was that he eventually earned enough money to buy a ticket so that his brother could join him. This always fascinated me. When I became interested in storytelling, I was moved to create a story about this important event in my family's past. But

I had little to go on. He had long since died, and my grandmother and mother had also died. I approached this problem
like an archaeologist. This snippet of a story was to me like a
pottery shard. Just as a good scientist can reconstruct the entire
pot from one piece, with my imagination I entered into this story
to re-create my grandfather's life. I did not approach this task
with the rigor of a genealogist or historian. Nor did I interview
other relatives to verify my facts. Rather, I decided to tell the
story as though I were my grandfather looking back in time.
What resulted was a performance piece called "The Ticket," in
which I reminisce about those early times. I even gave George
a fictional name—Morris Zivetsky.

Here was a thirteen-year-old kid living in an impoverished
shtetl in eastern Europe. I imagined that his brother had been
working hard to earn enough money to buy that ticket, and that
every day he filled George's imagination with tales of America,
a place where you could really be somebody. When he an-
nounced that he had bought the ticket, George couldn't resist.
He took that ticket and came to America instead.

This story came out of my sense of my grandfather as I knew
him. He was fiercely independent and knew how to survive. But
when I came to know him, he was a sickly old man who had re-
treated from life. These were the dynamic elements I attempted
to blend together in this story.

Not everyone in my family saw George in this way. My uncle
was angered and offended by my portrayal. I understand his reaction. George was a very different person for him—dashing,
stylish, well-dressed, and energetic. Nevertheless, my portrayal
still speaks to *me*, giving me a way of coming into relation with
a man who was not actively part of my childhood. I also recognize that in a fundamental way it has given me a chance to come
into deeper relation with the part of myself that wants to live
courageously, challenging life, grabbing the ticket, and running
for adventure.

You, too, can re-create the missing pieces of your life when there is no recourse except your fertile imagination. This does not mean that you should live in a fantasy world of your own creation. What you'll discover in these stories are the parts of yourself that are either dormant or waning. Your deepest desires and longings will appear in the lives of the family members you depict, revealing intimate truths about your family. Remember, even though not all of the stories you create are true, there will always be truth in them. Seek the truth and don't concern yourself with the minute and insignificant details.

Unfulfilled Needs

Looking back, there are many things I never got as a child that I desperately needed or wanted. Some fall in the category of material objects, and recalling them tells me a lot about myself as a child. One of my passions was pool. When I was nine years old, my uncle Sonny introduced me to the game by taking my cousin and me to Baker's Pool Hall. Baker's was in downtown Tampa next to the public library. The kinds of people who came in and out of its smoky, cavernous space filled with row after row of pool, snooker, and billiard tables were a different breed from those who frequented the book-lined floors of the library. It was anything but a quiet zone. Every few minutes someone would yell "Rack!," and Shine, a burly black man without a hair on his head, would rack the balls and collect ten cents for nine ball, a quarter for eight ball. From the first moment I picked up a pool cue, I loved the game. My sole obsession in life was to get a table at our house so I could play every waking moment. But we had no place to put one. With time I kept revising my wish until I was willing to settle for a small bumper-pool version that barely measured four feet in length. I never succeeded in convincing my parents that this was the one piece of furniture that would complement my mother's antiques. This was one of my childhood disappointments, but I doubt that it left any lasting scars.

At a more significant level are the things we never got that were crucial to our emotional and psychological development. We can carry some of these hurts to the grave and spend our life unwittingly trying to get other people to fill the yawning gap left by these unfulfilled needs. I spoke earlier of how I craved my father's attention, but rarely was rewarded. For most of my life, I have felt powerless to do anything about this loss. Each time I saw my father was a reminder of what I didn't receive. As an adult, I was still acting like the powerless child, waiting for something magically to change.

The first step in freeing myself from this story was to recognize that I was actually living within a story of my own making. My relationship with my father was like a dance in which I unconsciously decided to let him lead. After each song, I was dissatisfied with the style of the steps we took and where we ended up on the dance floor. But once the music started again, I would receptively raise my hands and proceed to let him again lead.

This pattern was set in motion fairly early in my childhood. I spoke earlier of my memory of a Saturday afternoon when my dad was taking a nap on the living-room couch. He was lying on his back with his mouth wide open, snoring. I wanted him to come outside and play with me. Sheepishly, I approached him and stood about a foot from his face, hoping that my mere presence would get him to open an eye. I had stood for what seemed like a long time when I heard my mother whisper from behind me. With her hand, she motioned to me to come in the other room. In hushed tones she admonished me for bothering my dad when he was so tired and worked so hard to give me so much. Sadly, I listened to her all too well. In my recollection, I rarely ever bothered him again with my needs and desires.

Now that I understand as an adult the dance I unwittingly agreed to all those years ago, I can decide to act differently with my primary relationships, including my dad. And I have chosen to do so with some success and satisfaction. If I don't like the tenor of what's happening with my relationship with my dad, I now take the lead. I speak what I feel and express what I want. For the most part, my father responds, although he isn't always surefooted.

Looking back . . . What are the things you missed as a child? What are the stories you tell about these losses? How have these stories perpetuated your inaction and belief that you are a victim? If you knew you could rewrite the current story, what would it look like? Regardless of your fantasy of how the other person will respond to your initiative, what would be your ideal scenario of how you'd like to act? Identify the thing you fear most about acting in this way. What is the worst thing that could happen if that occurred? Acknowledge this, but decide to act courageously in spite of the worst result you can anticipate. Remember, there is frequently more reward from giving love than in receiving it. To take the stance of choosing to love without expecting reciprocation is, I believe, the most empowering act we can undertake.

Facing Our Own Death

In the last analysis it is our conception of death which decides all our answers to the questions life poses to us.   —Dag Hammarskjöld

For many of us in this culture, this is the most difficult frontier of human experience. It's an area we rarely like to discuss, much less actively pursue. I, for one, have always had deep fears about dying. My earliest memory of my mortality goes back to age thirteen when I read *Death Be Not Proud*. It was a story about a precociously brilliant young boy who was diagnosed with a brain tumor. Valiantly he fought to live, but finally succumbed. This story gripped me for weeks. It was all I could think about. But I couldn't speak of my fears with anyone, not even my family.

As in most families in our culture, death and dying were taboo topics at the dinner table. I never even attended a funeral until I was in my twenties.

It's my belief, though, that until we come to grips with the meaning of our own mortality we cannot fully experience and appreciate the meaning of living. The first step is to ferret out the early stories we learned about death and dying. The lack of stories about this subject is relevant to understanding where we now stand regarding the transitory quality of our own being.

Looking back . . . Can you recall stories you were told in your childhood about the meaning of death? When pets or close relatives died, how was it explained to you? What were you told about where these loved ones had gone? Were heaven and hell described? Did you have a fear of dying? What did you imagine it would be like when you arrived in the next world? Did you expect to go to heaven or hell? What kinds of beings did you expect to find there?

Frequently, when we lose a parent, it sets an internal expectation that our death will follow a similar pattern. The father of one of my friends died at age fifty from cancer. From that time on, she dreaded reaching her own fiftieth birthday. There was no rational reason for her to believe that her fate would be the same, yet this fear persisted until she was fifty-one years old. Have you ever considered how old you will be when you die? Will you live to a ripe old age, or do you expect that you'll die young? What evidence do you have in your family that your genes predispose you in either direction? How do you see yourself dying? Will you be alone or surrounded by loved ones? Will it be a death filled with suffering or be relatively quick and painless? What is your vision of what awaits you once you die? Do you expect to be welcomed by all of your relatives who have passed on? If you believe that there is life after death, what is your best guess of what the next world will be like?

Facing the prospect of our own death has a way of helping us focus on life. Regrets and unfinished business will often be the first things that come to mind. If you knew you were going to die in twenty-four hours, what things would you want to say to the people who have been most important in your life? Have you allowed feelings, both positive and negative, to go unexpressed? What things have you done that you regret? Which accomplishments give you a sense of pride? Are there things you wish you could have done? Do you feel complete and accepting, or do you want to fight the prospect of leaving? Which stories about you would you want others to tell? What do you want to be remembered for? What has been your most important legacy?

Unfinished Business

Often, the fact that significant people in our lives have already died makes it seem more difficult to resolve past hurts that we suffered at their hands. They are no longer available to hear our stories, to ask for forgiveness, or to tell us about their pain and shame. In the following exercise, you'll be given a chance to both hear their distress and speak all the things you never felt safe enough to express.

THE SPECIAL ROOM

Imagine your dream home. It can have as many rooms as you like and is furnished to your exact taste. Attached to the house is a room with a separate outside entrance. This is your special retreat, which no one can enter except by your invitation. On the shelves are books and tapes filled with all the stories of your life, organized to your liking. There are two comfortable chairs in the middle of the room. You have total control in this room. People can speak only at your invitation. Otherwise, they must listen intently to the things you wish to say without commenting or defending their actions. *(Pause here for a moment to take time to imagine this place as vividly as you can.)*

Imagine that you are seated in one of the chairs when you hear a knock at the door. You get up and answer it. There on the steps in front of you is your mother. Whether or not your mother is still living, imagine her to be whatever age you choose. Invite her to come in and sit down. Join her in the opposite chair. Take a moment to look into her eyes. *(Pause here for a moment.)*

Now, in whatever way you like, tell your mother the many things that you could never express until this time. Of all the stories in your life, choose to tell her about those that involve her. Be sure to say what they meant to you. Your mother listens intently to every word you say, but does not respond or reply. This is your room, and she must listen without commenting or defending her actions. When you are finished, thank her for listening. Now invite your mother to share with you the things you would have liked to hear from her during your life. Imagine her speaking these things, as improbable as it may seem. *(Pause here for a moment.)*

What stories would you have liked to hear from her that you never heard? Imagine her sharing these with you now. *(Pause here for a moment.)*

If there is anything you would have liked to know about your mother, you can ask her, and she will gladly share it with you. Hear her voice. When you are finished and ready for her to go, thank her for listening and sharing with you, then ask her to leave.

There is another knock at the door. You get up and answer it. There on the steps in front of you is your father. Whether or not your father is still living, imagine him to be whatever age you choose. Invite him to come in and sit down. Join him in the opposite chair. Take a moment to look into his eyes. *(Pause here for a moment.)*

Now, in whatever way you like, tell your father the many things you could never express until this time. Of all the stories in your life, choose to tell him about those that involve him. Be sure to say what they meant to you. Your father listens intently to every word you say, but does not respond or reply. This is your room, and he must listen without commenting or defending his actions. When you have finished, thank him for listening. Now invite your father to share with you the things that you would have liked to hear from him during your life. Imagine him speaking these things, as improbable as it may seem. *(Pause here for a moment.)*

What stories would you have liked to hear from him that you never heard? Imagine him sharing these with you now. *(Pause here for a moment.)*

If there is anything you would have liked to know about your father, you can ask him, and he will gladly share it with you. Hear his voice. When you are finished and are ready for him to go, thank him for listening and sharing with you, then ask him to leave.

There is another knock. This time when you open the door, your spouse (or best friend) is standing in front of you. Invite this person to come in and sit down. Join him or her in the opposite chair. Take a moment to look into his or her eyes. *(Pause here for a moment.)*

Now, in whatever way you like, tell your spouse or friend the many things you could never express until this time. Of all the stories in your life, choose to tell him or her about those that are relevant to your relationship, and what they meant to you. He or she listens intently to every word you say, but does not respond or reply. This is your room, and this person must listen without commenting or defending his or her actions. When you are finished, express your thanks for listening. Now invite this person to share with you the things you would have liked to hear from him or her during your life. *(Pause here for a moment.)*

What stories would you have liked to hear from this person that you never heard? Imagine your spouse sharing these with you now. *(Pause here for a moment.)*

If there is anything you would have liked to know about your spouse, you can ask now, and he or she will gladly share it with you. Hear this person's voice. When you are finished and are ready for your spouse or friend to go, thank him or her for listening and sharing with you, then ask him or her to leave.

There is another knock at the door. This time, all of the significant people in your life are standing there. One by one, invite them in and repeat the above exercise with each. When you're finished, thank each person for listening and sharing with you, and then invite that person to leave.

There is one final knock at the door. This time when you open the door, God (as you understand God) is standing before you. Invite God to come in and sit down. Now is your opportunity to share with God your deepest feelings and thoughts. God patiently and compassionately listens to everything you have to say. Tell God about all the times you felt forsaken, forgotten, and alone. *(Pause here for a moment.)*

If there are things that have happened in your life that anger you, now is the time to share these things as well. *(Pause here for a moment.)*

If you choose, tell God about all the times you felt supported and loved, and thank God for this. Ask God to tell you how much he loves you. *(Pause here for a moment.)*

When you are finished and have expressed everything, offer your thanks and ask God to leave the room.

Take a few minutes to feel what it has been like to express these feelings and stories to all the important people in your life and to God. If you feel the desire, share with another person what this process was like, or write down your thoughts. If there are things you still feel unfinished about, and the person involved is still living, decide what, if any, appropriate things you would express to him or her. You may find it helpful to write these persons a letter before verbally telling them what's on your mind and in your heart. I have always found it helpful to ask myself whether telling someone what pains me about their past actions will improve or hurt our relationship. If I suspect that it's the latter, generally I've decided it is an issue that I best work out on my own.

Sometimes it is not just the past that requires healing and repair. Often, our present circumstances are missing ingredients to help make our lives fulfilling. In the coming chapter, we will explore how storytelling can be an elixir for enhancing everyday life.

CHAPTER 15

Tools for the Art of Living

Until now, our story journey has been focused on the distant past. It is not enough, though, to simply re-story the places where our deepest wounds reside. As a living and breathing part of daily life, story may help us discover the deepest and truest parts of our souls. By invigorating each day with the process of storytelling, we can find the sacred in the profane and can travel the path where our soulfulness is best revealed. We can also affirm the most positive aspect of our humanity while gaining perspective on those qualities in ourselves that are sometimes difficult to own, much less admire.

Building Your Self-Esteem

In one of the earlier exercises, we recovered an early experience of success. So many of us need to be reminded of our mastery of life. Unfortunately, it is often much easier to focus on our deficiencies, failures, lack of competence, and ineptitude. We now know that low self-esteem is learned from parents *and* educators who lack the understanding and skills to build positive self-concepts in children. The good news, though, is that low self-esteem is reversible, and storytelling may be one of the most powerful tools available for re-creating and sustaining positive feelings about yourself.

There are a few simple guidelines for assisting you in this journey. First, every day set aside time with your family or friends to tell a story about one achievement or thing you did successfully. As little as ten minutes will work. At first, you may find it difficult to uncover something that stands out. Most days are often commonplace and humdrum, and you may have an initial judgment that there is nothing consequential to share.

If you're stuck, begin describing your daily activities from the time you got up. As you proceed, ask yourself if there is anything you did that you once didn't know how to do. The answer, of course, is that almost everything you do now as an adult was at one time a new venture or a learning experience. Armed with this perspective, choose one thing you did today and tell about it as though you did it for the first time. You may feel foolish and even a little self-conscious. The goal, though, is to help you reframe the things you take for granted and appreciate yourself for performing these tasks as well as you do.

Those of you who are perfectionists will find that this practice sticks in your craw, and it's guaranteed to make you uncomfortable. But a great deal of good can come from confronting the part of yourself that denigrates even the most outstanding performances, much less the common, habitual activities of living. If you are willing to play with the process, you will have an opportunity to shift the abusive cycle that keeps you from experiencing deep satisfaction in your life.

These successes can encompass every aspect of your life. Whether you're a homemaker or the president of a bank, every day will present you with the opportunity to discover a reason to celebrate. And, as you know, hearing stories of others' successes can create an atmosphere in which you can share in the joy of achievement.

By making this a regular habit, you are building into the fabric of your relationships a powerful antidote to the negative drift that has engulfed our culture. The key here is repetition. Make it a practice to focus on success by telling stories that elevate even the seemingly insignificant details of your life to a place of sanctity filled with gratitude.

Stories of Strength

Each of us possesses certain strengths along with weaknesses. Unfortunately, most of us dwell on the things we don't do well. Not only does this damage our self-esteem, but such criticism also has little impact on our ability to correct our shortcomings. It just makes us feel bad. Yet we spend huge amounts of money and time attempting to fix our weaknesses. The assumption is that doing so will make everything all right. Research shows that the opposite is true. In *Soar with Your Strengths*, Donald Clifton and Paula Nelson present compelling evidence that fixing weaknesses creates average performance, not excellence. In fact, outstanding performance can be achieved only by focusing on the areas where we have strengths.

To identify your strengths, a good place to start is with the things that you enjoy doing most and the areas in which you learn quickly, both at work and in your personal life. If there are things at which you always excel, it's also a good bet that these are strengths. List at least six strengths. For each, tell a story about a situation in which this strength helped you create a positive outcome or success in your life. What are the details of what you did? How did you go about doing it? What was particularly satisfying?

Telling stories about our strengths can keep us focused on the things that help us succeed in life. Like all of the exercises in this chapter, connecting to events in our everyday experience that illustrate how our strengths have assisted us can keep alive our awareness of these key areas in our personality. Make it a point to regularly consider how your strengths got you through the day, and celebrate that accomplishment with the creation of a story.

Affirming Personal Values

All of us have values, but rarely do we identify these and look for ways to ensure that our external behavior is congruent with these internal touchstones. When we act in ways that contradict our deepest principles, even in small matters, we erode and tear at the fabric of our soul. If we go too far, we lose our center, our self-respect, and, no doubt, our regard for others.

The first step on this path is to identify and clarify what you stand for in the world. One way to do that is to complete the following statement: "It's important to me that . . ." You could conceivably generate hundreds of ideas in answer to this question, but start with the six things that are most important to you. For example, you might say, "It's important to me that I am always honest in my dealings with other people."

Another way to get to the things you value most is to consider the people who have been important to you in your life. What is it about them, the way they lived their lives, and their qualities, that you most admire? An example could be: "My aunt Faye was always taking us wherever we wanted to go when we were kids." Out of this model I could say that it was her generosity that impressed me the most.

List at least six people whom you admire. It's not necessary that you know them personally. They could be a movie star, a sports figure, a politician, or an artist. Next to their names, list what you admire most about them. If you were to synopsize each of these things into one word, what would the value be?

Whether you use the first approach or the latter, or a blend of both, narrow your list to six principles. For each of these, identify a potential story in your personal experience that reflects or embodies that value. These can come from any area of your life. For example, if one of your values was "to always give your very best," your story might be about a mentor at work who had an enormous commitment to excellence in every phase of the job, and how she performed every task with 100 percent attention to detail. These stories can be drawn from any time frame, even from childhood. And they needn't be long.

Not only can value-laden stories help us to clarify who we are, they can also become important guides for us and others when we are confronted by life demands that can implicitly pull us in directions contrary to our principles. Without telling the story, we may not recognize just how important these things are to us. And we may blindly proceed to numb ourselves to the implications of not honoring their validity. Like stories of success, it's important to continually remind ourselves of their importance by sharing stories in present time that illustrate and reinforce what we believe in. Without such stories, we and our children can become like leaves in the wind.

Keeping Our Word

While integrity is an important value, there is a form of dishonesty that is so universal and personal that it warrants special attention. Daily, weekly, monthly, and yearly we make promises to ourselves (and sometimes to God) that we nonchalantly break, only to renew the commitment again at a time of strength or remorse. I'm sure some of these will sound familiar. "This year, I'm going to start a regular exercise program." "I'm going to lose fifteen pounds this month so I can fit into a size eight." "As soon as I finish this project, I'll spend more time relaxing." And so on. Keeping our word with ourselves may be the most difficult thing we can accomplish. If we were to treat others with the same cavalier attitude, we'd have no credibility and few friends.

The importance of this question is not why we do this, but what can we do to enhance our own internal integrity? It's my belief that our self-esteem is intimately tied to this issue, although which causes what can be debated. Regardless, one way to address this issue is to identify times in your life when you have maintained your word and followed through on a personal commitment to yourself. Think of six such times and tell a story about each. Now identify the commitments you've made to yourself that are still in force. Each day that you are able to honor these, tell someone a story about how you did it. Turn it into a heroic tale. If, for example, your weight is an issue you'd like to address, and you've decided to forswear desserts, see yourself as the brave knight who went into battle with temptation, and triumphed. Make the chocolate cake into a dragon that you slew. Have fun telling the story.

If you failed, tell a story about how the brave knight was vanquished on the field of battle today, but how he has steeled himself in preparation for tomorrow's challenges. Find something redeeming in his behavior even if he did fail. Tell how he will succeed in the future when confronted by temptation.

These simple allegories can help us frame our difficult internal struggles and empower us in ways that self-recrimination can't. Through story, we can bring our private, internal war into an objective, shared arena. That place can often give us the leverage to make a shift, emboldening our inner resolve.

The Gift of Failure

> Last night when I was sleeping,
> I dreamt, thank God,
> That I had a beehive
> Inside my heart;
> And that the golden bees
> Were making

From my old and sad failures,
White combs and sweet honey.
    —Antonio Machado,
        "LIX—Last Night When I Was Asleep,"
        from *Solitudes, Galleries, and Other Poems,*
        translated by Maria M. Perez-Boudet

When a child takes his first steps alone, stumbles, and falls, we would never say he failed. Falling is all part of the learning process. In fact, we can never master any skill without stumbling. Unfortunately, our culture's educational system has subtly taught all of us that failing is a negative experience to be avoided at all costs rather than an opportunity to learn. When viewed from the latter perspective, failures can be seen as moments of empowerment that bring us ever closer to our goal. They can even be celebrated.

There are many examples and models from which to draw. Thomas Edison "failed" ten thousand times before he perfected the lightbulb. When asked if this had ever discouraged him, he replied that he saw every failure as a step that brought him closer to realizing his goal. Our national pastime, baseball, is another example. A player who strikes out two-thirds of the time is considered a superstar.

Reframing the meaning of our own shortcomings and failures can be an important step in our personal growth. It can also free us from the depleting drain on our energy that dwelling on mistakes brings.

On a sheet of paper or with a partner, share things that you failed at during your life. Describe briefly what happened and the short- and long-term effects of the failures. How did these things change your life? What did you learn from each? How did these failures subsequently help you?

Bringing this process closer to home, take time each week to consider one thing you failed at in the previous seven days. Tell the story about what happened. How can you reframe your description of this incident to see it as an important step in your own personal evolution? If you can't think of anything, then you're probably playing life too safe, and you aren't growing. Interestingly, the Chinese have one character for danger and opportunity. Seek out challenging situations. Learn from them. And celebrate when you stumble.

Finding Courage

To risk failure requires courage. As you probably know, "courage" is derived from the French word for heart, *coeur*. When we lose heart, the world seems forbidding, and we shrink from our own potential.

There are many ways in which story can help us return to our heart, and live with courage and zest. The first is through reminding us of the times when we readily embraced the opportunity inherent in every danger, and succeeded. Just last evening I was talking with my wife and lamenting the struggle involved in getting my seminar business off the ground. I had been feeling quite discouraged. She asked me to recount other times in my professional life in which I have encountered similar circumstances and have emerged without failing. In looking back, I could identify countless times that I faced grave situations— one of the largest clients in my advertising business declaring bankruptcy and leaving us holding the bag; returning to Florida without a job in the late seventies; selling my business and starting over without having a clear direction. In each case, I could see how my internal resources were more than adequate to guide me through dire straits that felt as if they would sink me.

When we concluded talking, I felt more at ease with myself for having been reminded of the fact that I have always been a risk taker and have always found a way to make my life work. My courage had been bolstered by these stories.

Looking back . . . Identify at least six instances in your own life in which you faced a real or perceived danger, and triumphed. What happened in each circumstance? What did you do that was courageous? How do the present dangers and fears in your life appear after telling these stories? How do you feel now?

Hearing others' stories of courage can also empower us. Their life stories can not only put our own difficulties into perspective, but can also provide models for alternative ways of seeing and acting. Many of the books listed in Recommended Reading are filled with such tales, and I encourage you to seek these out, read the stories, and share them with others.

In mythic terms, each time we courageously encounter the world, we are sharing in the age-old hero's journey. These stories began with a call to adventure. The hero or heroine was an ordinary person leading an ordinary life. Either through an inner prompting or the call of an outside person or force, our hero leaves home to encounter the unknown. But frequently, at first things don't go well. One danger after another engulfs the story's protagonist, and it's only through calling on his or her latent, inner strengths that the situation is transformed. In the process, new wisdom is realized, and the character returns home a changed person.

I believe the template for this journey is wired into the fabric of our souls. That's why we love to hear these stories. They touch that place in us where the spark of courage and adventure lives. We can also be "encouraged" by playfully making up fictional accounts of persons who faced grave physical tests or got into serious trouble, but through their intelligence, discovered a way out. Unwittingly, as wild and fictional as these stories are, they are also about us.

At your *Ceilidhs* or story-sharing circles, dedicate a night to fictional stories of courage. A favorite technique in our community is to have one person start the tale and progressively go around the circle, allowing each person to add to the story. At the conclusion, ask each person to reflect on what he or she learned from this tale. How is this story like a situation in your own life? How are the characters and their dilemmas analogous to your own journey and challenges? Remember, learning courage can be both fun and instructive.

The Miracle of Everyday Life

When I think about my many journeys into mountain wildernesses that are resplendent with brilliant sunsets and imposing mountain ranges, it's often simple things like our quiet times of sharing around the fire that I remember with greatest fondness. The everyday is constantly presenting us with these small gems. Thomas Moore suggests that we may discover what is best and deepest about ourselves in the banal aspects of our existence:

> To live with a high degree of artfulness means to attend to the small things that keep the soul engaged in whatever we are doing, and it is the very heart of soul making. From some grand overview of life, it may seem that only the big events are ultimately important. But to the soul, the most minute details and the most ordinary activities, carried out with mindfulness and art, have an effect far beyond their apparent insignificance.

There are a number of ways in which to enter into the ordinary and create a sacred altar from its details. For example, how we spend our free time can teach us a lot about our self and our personal journey. At the end of each day, talk about or write in your journal what you did during your time off. What did you see? Hear? Smell? Feel? In that quiet space, were you alone or with others? What did you talk about or do? If alone, what was it like to be silent?

Did something nice happen today? Was someone kind enough to keep a door open for you, or to help you pick up a bag of groceries that spilled onto the pavement? Did you do something nice for another person? How did it feel? How did they react? What nice thing did you do for yourself today?

My friend Paula Underwood makes a distinction between young eyes versus old eyes. Children can often see things we adults have become too jaded to perceive. An elder's vision is tempered by a lifetime of experience. This leads to a certain kind of wisdom. But a child's acute vision, which is free of the scars of living, can also be filled with its own brand of wisdom. For a five-year-old, a bug on a leaf can be a source of incredible pleasure and fascination. We adults would probably walk past the leaf and not really see the bug even if it was pointed out to us. A child can clearly see that the solution to her parents' fighting is forgiveness and love, but her parents can be so filled with self-righteousness that the simplicity of the solution escapes them.

Go for a walk and attempt to bring back the lucidity of seeing the world as a child. You needn't go far. In your own yard you could take a square foot of ground and watch closely everything that occurs there. You'll be surprised at the remarkable drama that can unfold when an ant attempts to traverse a forest of grass with the carcass of a bug twenty times its size. Now, there's a story worth sharing.

Overwhelming beauty is everywhere if we look: the morning dew on a spider's web; the veins of a dry, decaying leaf; even the shadow cast by a late afternoon sun as it shines through a window. Sometimes our experiences with nature can border on the miraculous. When I was hiking in Wyoming's Bridger Wilderness a number of years ago, we decided to take along fishing poles. Our destination, Island Lake, was heralded as a great place for trout. For nearly half an hour I cast my lure out into the water, only to reel it in without a bite. Then a trout hit and I knew I had the first catch of the day. And it was approaching dinnertime. But when I pulled the fish from the water, I was struck by its amazing beauty. It was, indeed, a rainbow. I suddenly felt remorse about taking this small trout's life. When I mentioned to my friends that the trout was puny and we should throw it back, they quickly protested that it was as big as anything they had ever seen served at a restaurant. I acquiesced and placed the fish on the rock at my feet. We continued fishing but had no more luck. It was time to clean my catch. My friend Ron and I took it down to the shore. Before I started, though, I asked forgiveness from the fish. I meant it. Proceeding quickly, I filleted it and tossed the head and guts back into the lake. Ron's wife joined us with a plastic bag and took the fillets back to the campsite. We decided to continue fishing for a few more minutes. That's when the magic happened.

After we cast out into the lake, a white gull appeared, circling over us. We were at ten thousand feet of elevation, and until that time hadn't seen any birds like this one. Nor did we ever see one again. The gull landed in the water about forty yards offshore, bobbing up and down for nearly five minutes. Then it took off and flew away.

I know there are many Native American stories that speak of how the soul of a departed animal is often transformed into that of another life-form. Was this gull the spirit of the trout? Was it just a coincidence? How do I explain this bird's remarkable appearance?

I don't know what this story means. It may be that in the telling and retelling it will be revealed, or part of myself that has been hidden will suddenly be unveiled as miraculously as the gull appeared out of thin air. This mystery is part of the adventure of living, and we must be open to the fact that some things simply must remain unknown. What things in your own life still live as mysteries? What things can't be explained away with simple science? How do you explain them? Consider applying the Rule of Six. It won't give you a definite answer, but it will help you grapple with the indeterminacy of it all.

Making Miracles with Stories

The world of spirit and miracle does not necessarily reside in a place different from where we are in this very moment. Sometimes, when we are weighed down by the pull of responsibility and managing the million and one small details associated with living in our society, we lose touch with the potential for miracles. In the Jewish Chasidic teachings, though, there's a profound belief based on Old Testament scripture that can give us an avenue back to that place of wholeness—if God hears prayers, he must also hear our stories. When we tell stories about our deepest spiritual experiences, or about the spiritual experiences of others, we can reenter the sacred space where spirit resides.

This can take many forms. It may be through the recounting of your faith journey. Each time you retell the story, it serves as a reminder of the healing quality of grace. And, since our body doesn't know the difference between the original experience and the imagined one expressed in our story, in a very real way we get to viscerally reexperience this deeply moving moment.

Another approach is to retell or read the stories of others' spiritual quests. By telling about the lives of holy people, we can benefit from their trials, tribulations, and breakthroughs. I have found that reading the twenty-fifth Psalm leads me into a very profound space of openness and gratitude. My tears are very real, and I'm deeply touched that this man thousands of years ago felt and expressed the very things that move within my own soul. Stories of the Chasidic masters, the Buddha, and Jesus can also evoke that same heartfelt reaction.

When my soul is bereft, I have found that it can be as easily filled and inspired by these stories as by prayer, song, and dance. Telling the story reignites the spiritual spark that lives in each of us.

Pitfalls and Vistas

The journey into story is always along a winding, bumpy path. For those of you who are willing to undertake this approach to developing the self, there are no promises that you'll reach a clearly defined destination. But it will be a trip of discovery filled with many rewards.

Pitfalls

I must warn you, though, that there are pitfalls and hidden snares that can divert you from the path and can even lead you to dangerous precipices. Sometimes, these are quite apparent, and you can catch yourself before it's too late. Often, though, when traversing difficult terrain without a trustworthy guide, we lose ourselves in the wilderness. My first piece of advice is that if you find yourself lost or stuck, or uncover a region of your past that is filled with unbearable pain, seek out a competent therapist or a good friend who knows how to listen. In my own life, there have been times of crisis that friends weren't equipped to handle, and I have found the guidance and support I needed from a professional. Likewise, my wife has provided me with the safety to explore painful aspects of my past that I had never spoken of before with friends or counselors. Trust yourself. You'll know when there are things associated with your stories that you and your friends can't handle alone.

There are many visible markers along the way that can help you identify when you're using story in a way that can hurt and obscure rather than reveal and help. Ironically, stories of hope are one genre that can be detrimental and even life-threatening. For example, if you have been having a recurring pain in your abdomen, you could spin a tale of how it's just indigestion or that's it's really nothing at all. You could even weave into the story your religious belief that "It's all in God's hands," hoping that He'll take care of you. Such a story could become quite dynamic. You could remember back over your life to other times when you have felt the same things and there was nothing wrong with you, or at the very most, it was inconsequential. This current event could be likened to those past occasions. Such a story filled with hope would certainly ease your anxiety and tension, but it could also disempower you and diminish your ability to courageously face what is going on. When story relaxes us in the face of fears that should be respected, it can keep us from action. Such stories are filled with denial, and they can cost us our lives.

Another version of this form of denial obscures rather than reveals our genuine experiences. When stories are grounded in fantasy rather than feelings and experience, they can keep us from adequately responding to the demands of the world around us. When I was fourteen, my school had the policy that if you failed to do an assignment, the teacher could report you to the headmaster and you had to go to a special study hall on Saturday. I had been ill and had called a friend to get the homework assignment. He neglected to tell me about part of it, and I was reported. I felt that it was unfair punishment, but the teacher would hear none of it. I decided, in protest, not to go to study hall, believing that I would be vindicated once my side of the story was told. My act of rebellion resulted in a suspension and the punishment of having to go to Saturday school for three weeks in a row. To say the least, I was caught up in my story of injustice and felt that the headmaster and everyone else in the school were jerks. I paid dearly for the story I told myself. It led me away from the truth of the situation, and was a denial of the consequences. When your stories result in greater pain, it's time to reevaluate and examine your assumptions. What are the beliefs underlying the stories you tell about yourself and others? How do you know they are true? When in doubt, apply the Rule of Six.

In a similar way, family stories can be used to perpetuate a lie, keeping us from facing the emotional truth of a situation. But like all lies, they often require additional lies to cover up the trail. Before long, duplicitous behavior like this can become the norm in a family, not the exception. Such stories need to be unmasked and exposed for what they really are. They're not simply one person's interpretation of a set of highly personal events. They're propaganda in its worst form, and a deep insult to our sense of integrity and honesty. While I have stressed that we must all have the latitude to reinterpret our pasts, we must also recognize that our stories need to be grounded in something real and authentic. In the final analysis, we must all be judges of the veracity of our stories, even when we're uncertain as to whether all the facts are true.

Ask yourself if your story is grounded in a deep truth and be willing to clearly acknowledge the "facts," which may or may not have happened as you remember them. Does the story reveal truth, or obscure it? Does it lead you to a greater sense of wholeness and integration, or does it require you to wall off part of yourself to ensure that the story's reality is never tested or questioned?

There is another side to this coin that must be considered. Sometimes, the reality of a situation is so horrific that we're better off not knowing the whole story. The truth of a situation and its probable implications can so immobilize us that we are consumed by our fears. Any chance for surviving may depend on how the story is told. For example, when an army is outgunned and outnumbered, if the commander told his troops the whole story, they could easily give in to their worst fears and stop fighting courageously. Certainly there are numerous examples in history when a small group of people triumphed in spite of overwhelming odds. What the troops don't know may save them.

We must also be cognizant of the fact that we are all highly suggestible. We can often embrace a story that sounds and feels true, but, in fact, isn't. For example, in a recent study by Elizabeth Loftus and Katherine Ketcham in *The Myth of Repressed Memory*, an older sibling was privately asked about three events that he or she knew the younger sibling had also experienced. Then, the researchers privately told the younger sibling what the older one had shared, but added a fabricated story about the younger sibling getting lost at the mall. They would then ask the younger child to tell about this event, and in nearly every case the child obliged them, in graphic detail. When informed that the event he or she had described was entirely fabricated, the young person could hardly believe the researchers. Even six months later the younger sibling still had a sense that the story he or she had told was true.

The consequences of most such stories is insignificant, but there are many cases in which suggested stories, if believed, can have dire implications for others. Unfortunately, it's nearly impossible to see through the veil of story to determine whether things really happened as we imagined them. When telling stories about others, beware of the potential for good and for harm. When in doubt, it may be best not to speak.

As much as I have emphasized the importance of telling and retelling our stories, I must also warn you that there are times when telling our story over and over again can actually be a symptom of the fact that we're stuck, and the story in its present form only continues the pain rather than lessening it. For example, one of the dominant stories in my early adult life was that I couldn't be successful in the world. Everything seemed intimidating—making a living, settling down and getting married, supporting a family, and sending children off to college. The tough thing was that I didn't have any evidence that I could do all those things. Now it seems strange to adhere to this belief given that I have overwhelming evidence to the contrary. But the story still has a place in my psychic life and can easily dominate my current view of myself and my capabilities to meet the challenges of life. To repeat this story does not free me. It only deepens the pattern of low self-esteem and perpetuates a painful personal myth. When your stories lead to this kind of behavior, they are not serving you. It's time to script a new tale.

Finally, there's a form of deadly self-righteousness that can show up in our stories. We must always be aware of the story we are living and be open to the possibility that our story may, in fact, be just that, resting on a foundation of shifting sands. This was most apparent to me during my work with the Foundation for Mideast Communication. In our workshops, people were asked to examine where they had learned their stories about the Mideast, Israel, the various wars, and the enemy. For most of us, we lived as though our stories were the truth. We weren't aware of the fact that they were stories, much less others' interpretations of the facts. What we found when we looked harder was that few of us had any direct experience. Our beliefs were based on hearsay. Even fewer of us had actually examined the historical records. The harder we looked, the more everything became quite murky and unsettling. There was no absolute evidence that could be used to create the broad and sweeping generalizations that characterized most of the debate and discussion on both sides of the fence. There were only stories that had been passed down and swallowed whole.

We needn't search far, though, to see how story can create

hatred and anger. Most of us needn't look farther than our own families.

What stories are you invested in that perpetuate painful conclusions and bitter feelings? What is the worst thing that would happen if you were to let go of your story and attempt to see the world from the other's point of view?

Vistas

As we conclude this journey, we come full circle to a new beginning. On my trips into the mountains, we'd never emerge from the trailhead feeling the same as when we started out. Always, I felt a desire to return, realizing that there were many paths we hadn't explored. Even trips in which I retraced my old steps were filled with new perspectives and things I had never noticed before. So it is with our own stories.

A number of years ago, a friend of mine gave me a tattered reproduction of a newspaper article that was no doubt many generations removed from the original. There was no attribution as to the author or the source. I want to share the essence of it with you because it illuminates so beautifully the essence of this book.

In the story, a woman was asked to describe the experience of raising a child with a disability. She likened it to preparing for a fabulous vacation trip to Italy. You buy all the guidebooks and make plans to visit all of the outstanding landmarks and works of art; you see yourself floating in a gondola in Venice and standing in awe in the Sistine Chapel; you can't wait for the day when your plane takes off and you set foot in this exciting foreign land.

Finally, the big moment arrives. Your bags are packed and your passport is in order. You board the plane and it takes off. But when you touch down, the stewardess announces that you have just arrived in Holland. "What do you mean?" you say. "I signed up for the first-class trip to Italy. This is not what I paid for."

The stewardess reassures you that you are in Holland, and that everyone must disembark. And, there are no return flights!

When you step out, you realize that it's not all that bad. In fact, there are many things Holland offers that you could never find in Italy. But there are a number of adjustments you must make. All that Italian you learned is no longer of any use. Now you have to learn a new language. And you've got to get new guidebooks. All the customs here are nothing like what you'd find in Italy.

While you experience the pain and disappointment of possibly never going to Italy, you discover that Holland has many redeeming features. This is not to minimize the loss of the dream, but if you don't get past your grief, you'll never be free enough to enjoy and relish the new journey you're on.

Even though I have emphasized throughout this book that we must actively embrace the authorship of our own stories, there are some things that are authored for us. They're out of our control. You can call it fate, destiny, the hand of God, or, simply, bad luck. This does not change the fact that some paths are one-way and that there is no return. How we accept these limitations will affect not only the story we tell, but, more fundamentally, our satisfaction and happiness. Through our stories we have an opportunity to embrace all that is, revealing the most noble and enduring facets of our humanity.

The Spoken Autobiography: A Questionnaire

Looking at the individual threads in the fabric of our lives can teach us a great deal about what made us who we are. But until we step back and look at the fabric as a whole, it's difficult to understand the overarching meaning and purpose of our lives. This is especially true when we grow older and it becomes more important to look back than to look forward. In my work with elders, I have found it useful to create a broad structure for this reflective process. I call it the "Spoken Autobiography," and it's designed for those of us who find it difficult to undertake this story journey alone. In my experience, I have found that it's frequently more comforting to have a fellow traveler along the road who is in some ways more interested in my life than I am. The probing, questioning, and curious listener can lead us deeper into our own stories, helping us to discover the meaning of our past and its relevance for the present.

Sam Keen and Anne Valley-Fox, authors of *Your Mythic Journey*, suggest that an important part of our spiritual journey is to write and rewrite our autobiographies many times throughout our lives. This process of self-reflection allows us to begin discovering the important themes that have woven their way into the tapestry of our life experiences. We can even catch glimpses of the powerful cultural and familial myths that have influenced our actions and decisions.

One way to begin is to ask yourself or the person you are inter-viewing, "What would be the major chapters of your life if you were to write your autobiography today?" You may gravitate to organizing your story chronologically, whereas others will be more predisposed to seeing their lives thematically. Go with whatever feels comfortable. After all, this is *your* story. What title would you give to each chap-ter? How would you describe the general action and key players in each? Don't go into detail here. Just look at the events as though you were giving a quick synopsis for a playbill. What title would you give to your life story today? Think of at least six, then choose one. What is it about this one that grabs you?

Now that you have a general structure, look at each chapter and explore in more detail all of the things that should be included. As you have seen from the exercises in previous chapters, all of life's ex-periences are fertile ground for interesting, thought-provoking, and moving stories that can heal, regardless of how ordinary or mundane the experience may seem at first. Anything that happened is fair game for a story, from events involving birth and death, high or low points in your family's history, humorous, even vulgar things that have hap-pened to one or more members of your family, stories that explain why your family does things the way they do, even the family name.

Here are some questions to help you or the person you're inter-viewing recall and identify important themes and experiences in your life. Before each section, I have included some of my own stories and thoughts to give you an example of the rich memories that can be dis-covered through the Spoken Autobiography.

In the Beginning

As a child, I was told our family name was really Steinwolf. No one is sure how it got changed. Perhaps it was the work of an impatient clerk on Ellis Island who couldn't understand my great-grandfather's heavy Russian accent. My guess is that he preferred something a lit-tle less ethnic. Even though this was America, I imagine my great-grandfather still harbored fears of persecution just because he was Jewish.

My mother's maiden name was Lindenbaum, which in German

means "linden tree." I never gave it much thought until recently, when I finished my first children's novel, which just so happens to be about giant creatures with trees growing out of the tops of their heads! I hope you find a piece of your history, and even identity, in the following questions about your family's origins.

FAMILY NAMES

Do you know whom you were named after? What do you know about this person? Do your names have any special meaning? Does your family name have a special history or meaning? Was it associated with a particular place in another country? Was your family name changed when your grandparents originally came to this country? What was it before? Is there a story about how it came to be what it is now? Are there any relatives with the old name? Do you have a family coat of arms?

FIRST SETTLERS

What are the names of the first of your family members to settle in this country? How did they get here? Where did they settle once they got here, and how many times did they move during their lifetimes? What brought them here? Did other family members already here help them come over? Where did they first arrive? Did they have any possessions, or did they come here with just the shirts on their backs? How did they make their livings? Did their children have to work? What difficulties did they experience?

THE OLD COUNTRY

Do you know any stories about life in the old country? How did your ancestors earn a living? Why did they want to leave their country? Was it famine or persecution? How about any folk stories from that country? What do you know about the folkways and customs of these people?

GRANDPARENTS

Do you know when and where your grandparents were born? Their full names? What did their parents do for a living? Do you have any pictures of them? How did your grandparents meet and marry? How old were they at the time? What difficulties or challenges did they have to face? Do you remember any of the stories about what life was like for them when they were younger? How did they come to choose the city where they lived? Were there any tragedies that affected their lives? What did they do to earn a living?

PASSING ON

When did the above relatives die? How did they die? Where are they buried? Have you ever visited their graves? What are the inscriptions on the tombstones? Did any of your relatives who would have been your uncles or aunts die as children? Do you know anything about their lives and how they died?

Family Legends

Lima, Ohio, is for some people a sleepy little town. For me, it's a place of excitement filled with mythic stories about my grandfather, my mother and father, and my uncle Sonny. Yet, through all these years, I have never visited Lima.

In the early 1930s, my grandfather went to Ohio seeking to buy a janitorial business, but was unsuccessful. On the train returning from Cleveland to New York, he met a man with whom he shared his difficulties. His newfound friend thought he could be of service. There was a man in Lima who was interested in selling. My grandfather bought that business, then sold it himself to move to Florida in 1949. My uncle Sonny was a teenager then.

Nearly forty years later, Sonny returned to Lima and bought back the business. The day he walked into the office, he found my grandfather's secretary sitting at the desk. Not missing a beat, she greeted Sonny as though he had left just yesterday! Perhaps there are similar legends in your family that have grown bigger with time. They're worth sharing and preserving.

PARENTS

What were your parents' full names? Do you know how they got those names? Where were they born? When? Where did they live during their childhoods? What kinds of things affected their personalities?

Did they come from a happy family or were there strife and difficulties?

MOM

What was your mother like? What are your fondest memories of her? Your earliest memory of her? What did you like most about her? Least about her? In what ways was your mother a perfect mom? In what ways did she fall short of your expectations? In what areas do you still feel pain in relation to her? What are the areas in which there's still unfinished business between the two of you?

DAD

What was your father like? What are your fondest memories of him? Your earliest memory of him? What did you like most about him? Least about him? In what ways was your father a perfect dad? In what ways did he fall short of your expectations? In what areas do you still feel pain in relation to him? What are the areas where there's still unfinished business between the two of you?

MAKING A LIVING

How did they make a living? Did you help them in their business when you were a child? Did your dad or mom ever lose their jobs? Were you aware of how much money your parents earned? Did you feel poor or rich?

AUNTS AND UNCLES

How many aunts or uncles did you have? What were their names? Are any of them still living? What do you remember about them? Were there any you were particularly fond of? What stories do you remember about them? Did you have any favorite relatives? What did they do to make them so special?

BROTHERS AND SISTERS

Did you have any brothers and sisters? What were their names and when were they born in relation to you? What was it like for you being in that position in the family? What were they like when you were growing up? Do you remember any special or funny stories about them? If you had older brothers or sisters, did they include you in their activities? Did your younger brother or sister tag along with you?

IDOLS
Whom did you look up to when you were younger? Why? How did you pattern your behavior after them? Were there any sports or movie personalities who were role models for you? Did an idol ever disappoint you? What happened? How did this affect the way in which you saw adults and the world?

Growing Up

It's a wonder that I didn't end up in a reform school! I recall standing on Eddie Smoak's balcony throwing eggs at passing cars, then hitting the deck when the irate drivers screeched to a halt and searched the bushes for us. We could see them, but they couldn't see us.

Before homemade weapons became a news item, we used to take CO^2 cartridges, bore them out, then fill them with match heads. We would shoot the projectiles through an iron pipe at Eddie's back wall. Our inventive bazooka was so powerful that it even scared us, and after the second trial we called off the experiment.

BIRTH
Were you born at home or in a hospital? When? Where? What do you know about your birth? How much did you weigh? Were there any complications? Were you a pretty baby? Whom did you look like? Were you breast-fed? What family members were present at the hospital or in your home? How many brothers and sisters came before you?

HOME
Where did you live as a child? What kinds of homes did you live in? What was your neighborhood like? What do you miss most about it? What do you not miss about it? What are some of your earliest memories? What positive or negative memories from your early childhood still stand out today?

LOOKS AND FEELINGS

What did you look like as a child? Did anyone ever tease you about your looks? Was there a particular feature that you couldn't stand? What was your favorite feature? Was your childhood happy, or difficult and sad? What kinds of trouble did you get into? Did you feel loved as a child?

SCHOOL

Who was your favorite teacher? The teacher you hated the most? What was your favorite subject? What subject did you like the least? What do you think was your most important lesson in school? Who were your best friends at school? How did you get to school each day? Did anything significant happen on these journeys? When did you stop going to school?

FIRST JOBS

What kinds of jobs did you have as a child? Which did you like the most? Did you learn any important lessons early on? What were your bosses like? Were you ever fired? How did you spend your money? What kind of job did you dream of as a child?

PASTIMES

What was your favorite pastime as a child? Did you play a musical instrument? Did your parents make you practice? What were your favorite games? Did you have a favorite pet? What was his or her name? Do you remember any stories about your pet? What was your favorite toy?

FRIENDS

Who was your best friend? What did you like and admire most about this person? Do you remember any stories about things you did together? Do you know where this person is now? Who were your enemies and whom did you hate? Who was the bully in the neighborhood? How did you deal with these people? Did you get into many fights? What happened?

UPS AND DOWNS

What are the happiest times you can remember? The saddest times? What happened? What things changed after that? Was there a major turning point in your childhood? How did this event change your life and that of your family?

LOSSES

Who is the first person you knew who died? Did any of your pets die when you were a child? Do you remember what happened? What other losses did you experience? Did you ever move and have to say good-bye to best friends?

LOVES

When is the first time you remember falling in love? What was the person like? What attracted you? Can you recall your first kiss? Did you go to dances with this person? What kinds of romantic things did you do? Did you go steady? Give the person a pin or a ring? If you broke up, what happened?

BELONGING

What groups did you join? Were there any special initiation rites? Did you belong to the Boy or Girl Scouts? What did you like most about these groups? Least? Did you join any sports teams? What positions did you play? What did you learn by being a member? What is your fondest memory of your participation?

Coming of Age

I left home when I was sixteen. My father decided that my education would best be served if I attended a prep school in New England. The long bus ride from the New York Port Authority to Springfield, Massachusetts, was the loneliest of my life. But, there were many wonderful things that came of my two years at Mount Hermon. My provincial views of the world were turned upside down as I became friends with kids from every part of the country, including the inner cities.

I remember during one blizzard challenging Ben Bullard to run four times around our giant dorm with nothing on but a T-shirt and pants; the giant food fight the night of our football loss to Deerfield Academy when Mr. Skib, the cook, served boiled potatoes; and Jack "The Hawk" Baldwin, the head of the English department, pointing a .22 caliber starting pistol at the entire school assembly to illustrate what the store manager must have felt when a group of seniors staged a fake holdup. Perhaps you, too, can remember the fear and anticipation when you finally left home and started making it on your own.

MENTORS

Who was the most influential person in your life? What did he or she do? How did you meet this person? What lessons did you learn? How did this person affect the rest of your life?

TEEN YEARS

What were your teenage years like? What was it like to go on your first date? Did you party a lot with your friends? When did you get your driver's license? Can you remember what that felt like? How about your first car? How were you rebellious? Did you get into any trouble? What kinds of discipline did you receive?

DREAMS

Did you have any goals or dreams as a young person? Did your family have any strong ideas about what you should do with your life? How did these change during these years?

COLLEGE

If you went to college, what did you study? Who were your best friends then? Did you belong to a fraternity or sorority? Did you participate in sports or other activities? What are your fondest memories? Were there any professors who made an impression on you?

WORK

How did you get your first job? Do you recall the job interview? How did that job lead to the type of work you do or did? What did you like the most about the different jobs you've had? The least? How much money did you make? Was it enough to make ends meet? Was money important to you then?

FAITH

When did you first formulate your own ideas about God? How did you see God at this time if you believed in his existence? How were your beliefs affected by your family and others you knew? How have these beliefs changed as you have grown older? Did you ever have a personal spiritual experience that changed the way in which you saw the world?

POLITICS

When did you first become aware of the political world? What's the earliest presidential election you can remember? Did you ever become actively involved in the political process as a child or young person? Who was your favorite politician? Did you ever run for office, either in your school government or in your community?

Making a Home

I came to marriage late in life. You might say that I made avoiding this commitment into an art. Yet, here I am with a four-bedroom house, a mortgage, a yard that needs mowing, innumerable chores, and a stepson who is teaching me a lot about patience. Why the wait? Recently we were watching *Zorba the Greek* with a group of friends. Alan Bates asks Anthony Quinn if he was ever married. Quinn replies, "Oh, yes, a wife, children, a house . . . the full catastrophe!" Elizabeth, my partner, smiled while I broke out in uncontrollable laughter. Every catastrophe has redeeming qualities. What about yours?

FIRST DATE

When did you first meet your husband/wife? Where were you? What was he/she like when you first met? What attracted you to him/her? Was it love at first sight? How long did you court? Did his/her parents like you? Did your parents like him/her? How old were you both?

MARRIAGE

Was marriage everything you expected it to be? What were your disappointments? What were the pleasant surprises? What was the most difficult thing to accept in the other person? What advice could you offer others about living together? Where did you and your partner first live? Describe it. How did you divide the chores? Was it hard to make ends meet? How did you make your living?

CHILDREN

How many children did you have? What were your feelings during the pregnancies and after your children were born? What do you remember about the birth of your children? Did you have any favorites? How did they differ from one another? Did you have any major disappointments with them? What stories can you remember about things your children did when they were very young? How was your life changed as a result of bringing them up?

ENDINGS

If you were divorced, what happened? What was good about that relationship? Bad? What is your biggest regret? If a marriage partner died, when did this occur, and how? Where is he or she buried? What is your fondest memory of your former spouse?

Taking Stock

From the tragedies and difficulties in our life we can learn many lessons. The following questions may help you discover and share these with those who matter.

WAR

Did you have to fight in a war? Which one? Were you wounded? Did you make any lifelong friends then? What is your most difficult memory about this time? Your most pleasant memory? Where were you stationed, and what was it like? How long were you in the military? What did you do after your discharge from the service? Was it difficult finding your footing? Who helped you out?

ACCIDENTS

Did you ever have a serious accident? What happened? How did this change your life? Were there some catastrophes that changed your life for the good?

GOOD TIMES, BAD TIMES

Looking back, what was the happiest time in your life? Why? What was the worst? If you had it to do over again, what would you change about your life?

ACHIEVEMENTS AND FAILURES

What have been the major accomplishments of your life? How did these affect the course of your life? What have been the major disappointments in your life? How did these affect the course of your life?

CHALLENGES

What has been the biggest challenge you faced in your life? How did you meet that challenge physically and emotionally? What did you learn?

JOURNEYS

Have you visited any wonderful places in your life? Tell me about them. Who accompanied you on these trips? What interesting people did you meet? What places would you never return to? Why? What place was the most beautiful?

FONDEST MEMORIES

What is your fondest memory? Why did you choose this particular experience? Who were the most important people in your life? Why? If you were to be remembered for one thing, what would that be?

RECOMMENDED READING

Akeret, Robert U. *Family Tales, Family Wisdom*. New York: Henry Holt and Company, 1991.

Barasch, Marc Ian. *The Healing Path*. New York: G.P. Putnam's Sons, 1993.

Bettelheim, Bruno. *The Uses of Enchantment*. New York: Vintage Books, 1977.

Bly, Robert. *Iron John*. Reading, PA: Addison-Wesley Publishing Company, Inc., 1990.

Brody, Ed, et al. *Spinning Tales, Weaving Hope: Stories of Peace, Justice & the Environment*. Philadelphia: New Society Publishers, 1992.

Buxbaum, Yitzhak. *Storytelling and Spirituality in Judaism*. Northvale, NJ: Jason Aronson, Inc., 1994.

Caduto, Michael J., and Joseph Bruchac. *Keepers of the Earth: North American Stories and Environmental Activities for Children*. Golden, CO: Fulcrum, Inc., 1988.

Campbell, Joseph. *The Hero with a Thousand Faces*. Princeton: Princeton University Press, 1949.

————. *Myths to Live By*. Toronto: Bantam Books, 1972.

Canfield, Jack, and Harold Clive Wells. *100 Ways to Enhance Self-Concept in the Classroom*. Boston: Allyn and Bacon, 1994.

Carter, Forrest. *The Education of Little Tree*. Albuquerque: University of New Mexico Press, 1976.

Cavanaugh, Brian. *More Sower's Seeds.* New York: Paulist Press, 1992.

———. *The Sower's Seeds.* New York: Paulist Press, 1990.

Chinen, Allan. *Once Upon a Midlife.* Los Angeles: Jeremy P. Tarcher, Inc., 1992.

———. *In the Ever After: Fairy Tales and the Second Half of Life.* Wilmette, IL: Chiron Publications, 1991.

Dass, Ram, and Paul Gorman. *How Can I Help?* New York: Alfred A. Knopf, 1994.

Davis, Donald. *Telling Your Own Stories.* Little Rock: August House Publishers, 1993.

Estés, Clarissa Pinkola. *The Gift of Story.* New York: Ballantine Books, 1993.

———. *Women Who Run with the Wolves.* New York: Ballantine Books, 1992.

Feldman, Christina, and Jack Kornfield, *Stories of the Spirit, Stories of the Heart.* New York: HarperCollins, 1991.

Frankl, Victor. *Man's Search for Meaning.* New York: Simon & Schuster, 1984.

Gardner, Richard. *Storytelling in Psychotherapy with Children.* Northvale, NJ: Jason Aronson Inc., 1993.

Goldberg, Natalie. *Wild Mind: Living the Writer's Life.* New York: Bantam Books, 1990.

———. *Writing Down the Bones.* Boston: Shambhala, 1986.

Henderschedt, James L. *The Magic Stone and Other Stories for the Faith Journey.* San Jose, CA: Resource Publications, 1989.

Jackowski, Karol A. *Ten Fun Things to Do Before You Die.* Notre Dame: Ave Marie Press, 1989.

Keene, Sam, and Anne Valley-Fox. *Your Mythic Journey.* Los Angeles: Jeremy P. Tarcher, Inc., 1989.

Klauser, Henriette Anne. *Writing on Both Sides of the Brain.* New York: HarperCollins, 1987.

———.*Put Your Heart on Paper.* New York: Bantam, 1995.

Kline, Nancy. *Women and Power: How Far Can We Go?* London: BBC Books, 1993.

Krohn, Paysach J. *Around the Maggid's Table.* Brooklyn: Mesorah Publications, 1992.

————. *In the Footsteps of the Maggid*. Brooklyn: Mesorah Publications, Ltd., 1992.

————. *The Maggid Speaks*. Brooklyn: Mesorah Publications, 1990.

Kurtz, Ernest, and Katherine Ketcham. *The Spirituality of Imperfection*. New York: Bantam Books, 1994.

Livo, Norma, and Sandra Rietz. *Storytelling Activities*. Littleton, CO: Libraries Unlimited, Inc., 1987.

————. *Storytelling: Process & Practice*. Littleton, CO: Libraries Unlimited, 1986.

MacDonald, Margaret Read. *Peace Tales: World Folktales to Talk About*. Hamden, CT: Linnet Books, 1992.

Maguire, Jack. *Creative Storytelling*. New York: McGraw-Hill Book Company, 1985.

Mander, Jerry. *In the Absence of the Sacred*. San Francisco: Sierra Club Books, 1991.

Margolis, Vivienne, Kerry Smith, and Adelle Weiss. *Fanfare for a Feather*. San Jose, CA: Resource Publications, 1991.

Maybury-Lewis, David. *Millennium: Tribal Wisdom and the Modern World*. New York: Viking, 1992.

McAdams, Dan P. *Stories We Live By*. New York: William Morrow and Company, 1993.

de Mello, Anthony. *The Song of the Bird*. New York: Doubleday, 1982.

————. *Taking Flight: A Book of Story Meditations*. New York: Image Books, 1988.

Mellon, Nancy. *Storytelling & the Art of Imagination*. Rockport, MA: Element, 1992.

Miller, Teresa. *Joining In: An Anthology of Audience Participation Stories & How to Tell Them*. Cambridge: Yellow Moon Press, 1988.

Moore, Robin. *Awakening the Hidden Storyteller*. Boston: Shambhala, 1991.

Moore, Thomas. *Care of the Soul*. New York: HarperPerennial, 1992.

Papineau, Andre. *Jesus on the Mend: Healing Stories for Ordinary People*. San Jose, CA: Resource Publications, 1989.

Pellowski, Anne. *The Family Storytelling Handbook*. New York: Macmillan Publishing Company, 1987.

————. *The Story Vine.* New York: Collier Books, 1984.

Plato. *Phaedrus and Letters VII and VIII.* London: Penguin Books, 1973.

Roads, Michael. *Talking with Nature.* Tiburon, CA: HJ Kramer Inc., 1987.

Schachter-Shalomi, Zalman. *From Age-ing to Sage-ing.* New York: Warner Books, 1995.

Schram, Peninnah. *Tales of Elijah the Prophet.* Northvale, NJ: Jason Aronson, Inc., 1991.

Seed, John, Joanna Macy, Pat Fleming, and Arne Naess. *Thinking Like a Mountain.* Philadelphia: New Society Publishers, 1988.

Simpkinson, Charles, and Anne Simpkinson. *Sacred Stories: A Celebration of the Power of Stories to Transform and Heal.* San Francisco: HarperCollins, 1993.

Storm, Hysmeyohsts. *Seven Arrows.* New York: Ballantine Books, 1972.

Thorsheim, Howard, and Bruce Roberts. *Reminiscing Together.* Minneapolis: CompCare Publishers, 1990.

Underwood, Paula. *Three Strands in the Braid.* San Anselmo, CA: A Tribe of Two Press, 1984.

————. *The Walking People.* San Anselmo, CA: A Tribe of Two Press and Institute of Noetic Sciences, 1993.

————. *Who Speaks for Wolf?* San Anselmo, CA: A Tribe of Two Press, 1991.

de Vos, Gail. *Storytelling for Young Adults—Techniques and Treasury.* Englewood, NJ: Libraries Unlimited, Inc., 1991.

Wakefield, Dan. *The Story of Your Life: Writing a Spiritual Autobiography.* Boston: Beacon Press, 1990.

White, Michael, and David Epston. *Narrative Means to Therapeutic Ends.* New York: W.W. Norton & Company, 1990.

Wiesel, Elie. *Messengers of God: Biblical Portraits and Legends.* New York: Summit Books, 1976.

————. *Somewhere a Master—Further Chasidic Portraits and Legends.* New York: Summit Books, 1982.

————. *Souls on Fire—Portraits and Legends of Chasidic Masters.* New York: Summit Books, 1972.

Williams, Michael E. *Friends for Life: A Treasury of Stories for Worship and Other Gatherings.* Nashville: Abingdon Press, 1989.

Zevin, S.Y. *A Treasury of Chassidic Tales on the Festivals,* vol. 2. Brooklyn: Mesorah Publications, 1982.

————. *A Treasury of Chassidic Tales on the Torah,* vol. 1. Brooklyn: Mesorah Publications, 1980.

————. *A Treasury of Chassidic Tales on the Torah,* vol. 2. Brooklyn: Mesorah Publications, 1980.

National Storytelling Association
P.O. Box 309
Jonesborough, TN 37659
615-753-2171
A national clearinghouse for storytelling resources and activities throughout the country. NSA is largely responsible for the renaissance of storytelling in this country during the last twenty years, and sponsors the annual National Storytelling Festival held the first weekend of October.

The Past Is Prologue Education Program
P.O. Box 216
San Anselmo, CA 94979
415-457-6548
Paula Underwood developed this program, and it is based on the learning model that is discussed in chapter 13. PIP is designated as an "Exemplary Educational Program" by the U.S. Department of Education, and is being used in schools and corporations throughout the United States.

StoryWork Institute
P.O. Box 941551
Maitland, FL 32794-1551
407-767-0067
This is the author's organization, which sponsors training programs for healthcare professionals nationwide.

ABOUT THE AUTHOR

Richard Stone has been a national leader in the development and application of training programs for counselors, social workers, nurses, chaplains, hospice professionals, and healthcare volunteers. His program "Journey Into the Healing Power of Storytelling" has been used to facilitate the life-review process for patients and their families and to teach professionals how to bring the practical applications of storytelling into their therapeutic work. In addition, his program "Healing the Family Circle Through the Art of Storytelling" has been offered through churches, synagogues, and other institutions committed to strengthening family ties.

Under the auspices of the StoryWork Institute, which he founded in 1993, Mr. Stone has developed training programs for team building, leadership development, and diversity training for organizations and healthcare institutions. Currently, he is consulting with one of Florida's largest hospital systems, helping it to create a system for collecting and disseminating positive patient-care stories. The program is called "Healing Stories."

He also has been a featured presenter at the National Hospice Organization's Leadership Development Conference and Spiritual Caregivers Conference, and has served as an adjunct professor at the University of Central Florida and Valencia Community College, where he taught courses on the uses of storytelling as a transformational tool. His recent book, *Stories: The Family Legacy,* is a guide for sharing and recollection, and is being used by hospice and healthcare professionals throughout the U.S. He lives in Maitland, Florida.